# Lucy and the
# Piano Player

**Elizabeth Neblett**

PEARSON
Longman

**Modern Dramas 2: Lucy and the Piano Player**
**First Edition**

Copyright © 2008

Pearson Education, Inc.
10 Bank Street, White Plains, NY 10606

**Staff credits:** The people who made up the *Modern Dramas 2: Lucy and the Piano Player* team, representing editorial, production, design, and manufacturing, include Pietro Alongi, Ann France, Laura Le Dréan, Martha McGaughey, Jaime Lieber, Michael Mone, and Edie Pullman.

**Cover illustration:** Don Dyen, Wilkinson Studios
**Text design:** Jimmie Young, Tolman Creek Design
**Text composition:** S4Carlisle Publishing Services
**Text font:** 12.5/13 Minion
**Illustrations:** Don Dyen, Wilkinson Studios

ISBN-13: 978-0-13-242336-6
ISBN-10: 0-13-242336-7

**LONGMAN** ON THE **WEB**

**Pearsonlongman.com** offers online resources for teachers and students. Access our Companion Websites, our online catalog, and our local offices around the world.

Visit us at **www.pearsonlongman.com**.

Printed in the United States of America

1 2019

# Contents

# To the Teacher

*Lucy and the Piano Player* is the second book in the series of four Longman *Modern Dramas*. These dramas provide authentic, level-appropriate, engaging literature for adult English language learners. The individual episodes of the books can either stand alone or be taught in sequence as part of an ongoing course. *Modern Dramas* fill the need in the beginning to low-intermediate classroom for controlled reading material of more than a few paragraphs. *Modern Dramas* also keep the students interested in what they are reading: They will want to keep turning the pages to find out what happens next.

You will be amazed at how engaged your students will be with these stories. The involving story lines will draw students in, and motivate them to keep on reading. The language is not completely grammatically controlled; *Modern Dramas* aim above all to be interesting and natural, and have been written with an eye to research that shows that most students' reading ability is at a higher level than their speaking, listening, or writing skills. By the last episode, your students will be able to follow the plot and to answer the reading comprehension questions without using their dictionaries.

In this second book of the series, eleven episodes follow the story of Lucy Karbowski as she adjusts to life in a new city, copes with her job and her mother, and hopes to find true love. Students learn vocabulary related to daily-life skills and issues.

Each of the eleven episodes consists of:

- **The opening page**
  A picture sparks student interest in the episode to come, and provides a springboard for lively student discussion.

- **Get Ready to Read**
  The two questions about the opening art can be discussed in pairs, small groups, or with the whole class. These questions focus students' attention on the theme of the episode. An exercise after these questions introduces new vocabulary.

- **In the last episode . . .**
  Each episode starts with a brief summary of the previous episode, so that students who were absent will be able to follow the story, and students who have been in class will be reminded of what has already happened.

- **The reading**

  Each reading is between 600 and 1,000 words. You can assign the episode and the exercises following it for homework, but it is also useful to read it aloud to the class, or to have the students listen to the recording of the episode before they read it on their own. New vocabulary not targeted on the opening page is defined either with small illustrations or with a gloss on the relevant page.

- **Reading Comprehension**

  These true/false and multiple-choice questions check students' understanding of what they have just read. The exercises can be used for class discussion. You can encourage students to explain their answers or tell the class where in the episode they found the information to answer the questions.

- **Work with the Words**

  These exercises review and solidify students' knowledge of new vocabulary, both the words targeted on the opening page and other vocabulary words which have come up in the reading. The exercises are multiple choice, fill in the blank, and select the opposite word, among others.

- **Lifeskill Practice**

  These exercises focus on a particular theme or competency featured in the episode. The exercises reinforce standard life skills and competencies.

- **Dialogue Practice**

  Selected portions of the episode are reproduced at the end of each of the nine segments so that students can practice the language in a focused way. These can be used for pronunciation practice or role play.

After your students finish *Lucy and the Piano Player*, they will be eager to read the other books in the *Modern Dramas* series: *Solomon the Superintendent*, *Victor's Secret*, and *Ramona's Adventure*.

# A New City

Episode 1

# Get Ready to Read

**A**  Discuss with a partner.

1. Find Chicago on the map. Find Silicon Valley on the map.
2. Lucy is a single working woman. What is her job?

**B**  Match the words with the definitions.

_c_ **1.** loan

_f_ **2.** client

_a_ **3.** opportunity

_g_ **4.** colleague

_b_ **5.** originally

_d_ **6.** convenient

_e_ **7.** sociable

**a.** chance

**b.** first; in the beginning

**c.** money you get from a bank; you must pay it back

**d.** easy to use; practical

**e.** friendly

**f.** customer

**g.** coworker

## About Lucy

Lucy Karbowski lives in Silicon Valley. Silicon Valley is in California, near San Francisco. Many high-tech companies, for example, Xerox, IBM, and Apple have offices there.

Lucy Karbowski works at a bank for Internet companies, in San Jose. She is a **loan** officer. She meets with new **clients**, answers their questions, and helps them with the applications. Later she discusses the company with her **colleagues**, and they decide if the bank will give the company a loan. Lucy loves her job. She has the **opportunity** to travel a few times a year. She has her own office. She is happy with her salary and the **benefits**,* but she works very hard, sometimes ten hours a day. Lucy is attractive. She has blue eyes and brown hair. She's about 5 feet, 2 inches tall, and she is medium weight. Now she's 28 years old, and she's beginning to think about marriage. The problem is that Lucy doesn't have many opportunities to meet single men.

*benefits = (from a job) health insurance, vacation time, time off

Lucy Karbowski is **originally** from Chicago, Illinois. After she finished college, she moved back in with her parents to save money. Then she decided to go to graduate school for a master's degree in computer science. Lucy was a very serious student and received excellent grades, but she didn't have time for a social life. She studied all the time and worked part-time at a video store to pay for college.

After Lucy finished her studies, a bank offered her a job in downtown Chicago. It was **convenient** to her home, and the salary and benefits were good. She worked there for four years. Then her father died, and everything changed. Lucy's mother began to talk to Lucy about marriage and grandchildren. Every week, Lucy's mother tried to introduce Lucy to men who lived in the neighborhood. Sometimes she called Lucy at work. This was a typical conversation:

| | |
|---|---|
| **Mrs. Karbowski:** | Lucy, are you going to be home early tonight? |
| **Lucy:** | I don't know, Mom. Why? |
| **Mrs. Karbowski:** | There's someone that I want you to meet. |
| **Lucy:** | Again? Who is it this time, Mom? |
| **Mrs. Karbowski:** | It's Mrs. Walker's son, John. He's a doctor, you know. |
| **Lucy:** | But, Mom, he's 50 years old! Wasn't he married before? |
| **Mrs. Karbowski:** | Well, yeah, he was married three times. |
| **Lucy:** | Three times? Forget it. |
| **Mrs. Karbowski:** | But, Lucy, he's a doctor! |
| **Lucy:** | Bye, Mom. I'll talk to you later. |

Lucy wasn't interested in any of the men. They all wanted Lucy to quit her job, stay at home, and raise a family. Lucy was interested in marriage, but she wanted a career, too. A year later, Lucy's brother, Paul, invited Lucy and their mother to move to Portland, Oregon, where he was living. Lucy's mother decided to sell the family house and move. Lucy's bank didn't have an office in Portland, but it had a West Coast office in San Jose, California. Now Lucy is comfortable at the new office, and she's happy that her family is not too far away. She's also happy that her mother isn't there watching her all the time, but sometimes Lucy is a little lonely because she doesn't have time to meet new people.

**colleague**

Lucy's **colleague** Anna Tanaka works in the office next door, and she is Lucy's best friend. She likes to talk, and she always invites Lucy to go out. Anna is more **sociable** than Lucy, and she can't understand why Lucy doesn't go out more. Tonight she has an idea for Lucy.

It's late, about eight o'clock at night, and Lucy is at work. Anna comes into Lucy's office.

"Come on, Lucy. Let's go get something to eat."

"OK. Give me five more minutes," Lucy says.

"Uh . . . Lucy. You know, you always work late. You need to meet some new people. Everybody that you know works here at the bank."

"I know, but I'm very busy. I don't have time to go out."

"You're young. You're single. You're attractive. You have a good job, but you need to go out more."

"Where? To bars? To discos? Forget about it! I want to meet a nice man. I want a nice man who's not too tall and not too short. I want to meet a **handsome**\* man who's intelligent and has a good job. I don't want an old man, but I don't want a very young man. It's difficult to find someone like that."

---

\***handsome** = good-looking, attractive

Anna says, "Really? Well, I think I have the perfect man for you, Lucy. His name is Michael Benson. I gave him your phone number. He's going to call you tomorrow."

"What? Tomorrow?"

# Reading Comprehension

**A**  Circle *True* or *False*.

|   |   | | |
|---|---|---|---|
| 1. | Silicon Valley is in California. | True | False |
| 2. | There are many high-tech companies in Silicon Valley. | True | False |
| 3. | Lucy is originally from California. | True | False |
| 4. | Lucy sometimes travels for her job. | True | False |
| 5. | Lucy's family lives in San Jose. | True | False |
| 6. | Lucy's brother and mother live in the same city. | True | False |
| 7. | Lucy has many friends in San Jose. | True | False |
| 8. | Lucy's bank has offices in Portland and San Jose. | True | False |

**B**  Circle the correct answer.

1. Lucy has _____.
   a. brown eyes and brown hair
   b. blue eyes and brown hair
   c. brown eyes and blonde hair
   d. blue eyes and blonde hair

2. Lucy knows Anna from _____.
   a. Chicago
   b. Portland
   c. high school
   d. work

3. Lucy wants to _____.
   a. get a new job
   b. go back to Chicago
   c. meet a nice man
   d. stay single

4. Lucy's mother wants Lucy to _____.
   a. go back to college
   b. stay single
   c. get married
   d. work harder

5. Anna wants Lucy to _____.
   a. introduce her to a nice man
   b. meet a nice man
   c. work more hours
   d. eat breakfast

# Work with the Words

**A** Circle the correct answer.

1. I need a new car, but I don't have enough money. I'm getting a
   _____ from the bank.
   a. check
   b. colleague
   c. benefits
   d. loan

2. Who has **clients**?
   a. a teacher
   b. a doctor
   c. a bank officer
   d. a police officer

3. *Lucy has the* **opportunity** *to travel* means
   a. Lucy can travel.
   b. Lucy doesn't travel.
   c. Lucy likes to travel.
   d. Lucy cannot travel.

4. I don't drive. Which job is **convenient** for me?
   a. The office is one hour away by car.
   b. The office is a ten-minute walk.
   c. The office is not near public transportation.
   d. A bus stop is twenty minutes from the office.

5. A **sociable** person likes to _____.
   a. be with friends
   b. stay home alone
   c. work alone
   d. travel by herself

6. *Lucy is* **originally** *from Chicago* means
   a. Lucy didn't live in Chicago.
   b. Lucy was born in Chicago.
   c. Lucy likes Chicago.
   d. Now Lucy lives in Chicago.

7. A teacher's **colleague** is _____.
   a. the principal
   b. a student
   c. another teacher
   d. the custodian

8. His job has good **benefits**. He _____.
   a. has good health insurance
   b. doesn't work at night
   c. works at night
   d. has a big office

**B** Complete the sentences. Use the words in the box.

| benefits | convenient | opportunity |
|----------|------------|-------------|
| client | handsome | originally |
| colleague | loan | sociable |

1. Lucy is _originally_ from Chicago.

2. Lucy is helping a _client_ with his loan application.

3. Anna wants to buy a house. She needs a _loan_ from the bank.

4. Lucy's office location is _convenient._ It's only a short bus ride from her home.

5. Anna likes to talk, and she goes out every night. She is very _sociable_ .

6. Lucy says she wants to meet a _handsome_ man.

7. Lucy likes her job because she has the _opportunity_ to travel.

8. Anna and Lucy work in the same office. Anna is Lucy's _colleague_.

9. I have three young children. I don't want to take a job without _benefits_ .

# Lifeskill Practice

Use *Let's* when you have a good idea.
Anna says, "**Let's** go get something to eat."

Complete the sentences.

You are hungry. It's lunchtime. What do you say to your friend?

1. Let's _go to eat_ .

Your family is ready for dinner, but you don't want to cook tonight. What do you say?

2. Let's _____ .

# Dialogue Practice

Practice the conversation with a classmate.

**Anna:** Come on, Lucy. Let's go get something to eat.

**Lucy:** OK. Give me five more minutes.

**Anna:** Uh . . . Lucy. You know, you always work late. You need to meet some new people. Everybody that you know works here at the bank.

**Lucy:** I know, but I'm very busy. I don't have time to go out.

**Anna:** You're young. You're single. You're attractive. You have a good job, but you need to go out more.

**Lucy:** Where? To bars? To discos? Forget about it! I want to meet a nice man. I want a nice man who's not too tall and not too short. I want to meet a handsome man who's intelligent and has a good job. I don't want an old man, but I don't want a very young man. It's difficult to find someone like that.

**Anna:** Really? Well, I think I have the perfect man for you, Lucy. His name is Michael Benson. I gave him your phone number. He's going to call you tomorrow.

**Lucy:** What? Tomorrow?

# A Blind Date

# Get Ready to Read

 **Discuss with a partner.**

1. What is a "blind date"?

2. Lucy is going to ask Anna some questions about her blind date, Anna's friend Michael. What questions will Lucy ask? Make a list with your partner.

**B** Match the words with the definitions.

<u>f</u> 1. luxury            **a.** far away

<u>c</u> 2. athletic           **b.** make money

<u>B</u> 3. earn               **c.** likes to exercise or play sports

<u>e</u> 4. in good shape     **d.** not good-looking; not beautiful

<u>G</u> 5. salary            **e.** strong; not fat or too thin

<u>A</u> 6. long-distance     **f.** expensive

<u>D</u> 7. ugly              **g.** regular money for your work

## In the last episode...

Lucy is a single woman. She is new in San Jose, California. She has a good job as a loan officer at a bank. Lucy works very hard, and she is an attractive young woman, but she doesn't have time for a social life. She is starting to think about marriage, but she doesn't know many single men. Her coworker and friend, Anna Tanaka, gave Lucy's phone number to a friend. She wants Lucy to go on a blind date!

Lucy wants to meet a nice, single man. She wants to meet a man who is not too old but not too young, not too tall but not too short. She wants a handsome man with a good job. She wants a lot!

Lucy's best friend at work, Anna, thinks that she has the perfect man for Lucy. His name is Michael. Anna gave Michael Lucy's phone number, and he is going to call Lucy tomorrow. Lucy can't believe it!

"Anna, are you crazy? Who is this man? What's his name? Marc?"

"His name is Michael Benson. Don't worry, Lucy. He's very nice."

"Really? How do you know him?"

"He's my brother's best friend."

"How old is he?"

"He's 31 years old."

"Where is he from? Is he American?"

"That's a strange question. Yes, I think he's American."

"Where does he live? I don't want a **long-distance** relationship."

"He is originally from Los Angeles, but now he lives here in San Jose. He lives in a **luxury** apartment building. My brother is one of his neighbors."

"What does he do? Where does he work?"

"He works at a law office down the street. He's a computer programmer there."

"A computer programmer? Hmm. What does he look like? How tall is he? Is he **ugly**?"

"Ugly? No, he's very attractive. He's 6 feet, 1 inch tall, and he weighs about 190 pounds. He has short, **wavy** black hair. He has brown eyes."

Lucy is a little more interested. "Hmm. Does he make good money?"

"He **earns** a good **salary**, Lucy. He is **in charge of**[*] his department. My brother says that he has a master's degree, too."

"That's good. Is he quiet?" Lucy asks.

"No, he's talkative, and he's very friendly."

"Does he like music?" Lucy asks.

"Yes. Michael likes all kinds of music: jazz, reggae, classical, and hip hop, too. He's learning how to play the guitar, too. Oh, and he's a great dancer. I saw him at a club."

Lucy thinks to herself, "He's a good dancer? I love to dance!" but she doesn't say anything to Anna. She asks another question: "Is he **in good shape**?"

"Of course he is. He likes sports. He and my brother play basketball together. He's very **athletic**. He runs every morning, and he goes to a **gym**[**] every evening after work."

"Does he like to travel? You know, Anna, I like to travel to interesting places."

"I think so. My brother told me that he went to Australia last winter."

"Maybe he's too perfect," Lucy thinks. Then she asks Anna: "Why don't you go out with him?"

"You know about my boyfriend, Jim. But Michael is really perfect for you, Lucy. Any more questions?"

"OK, OK. Last question. Is he looking for something serious?"

"He's talking about marriage, too. Well, do you want to meet him?"

**straight**

**curly**

**wavy**

---

[*]**in charge of** = manages, is responsible for

[**]**gym** = a health club; a place where people go to exercise

"Mmm. OK. Maybe it will be interesting to meet someone new."

"OK, Lucy. He wants to meet you, too. Michael will call you tomorrow. Please be nice. He's really perfect for you."

\*   \*   \*   \*

It's five o'clock the next day, and Lucy is at work. She is very excited, but she is very nervous, too. This is her first blind date. She doesn't have a picture of Michael, but Anna told her everything about him. The telephone rings. Lucy quickly answers.

"Hello. Lucy Karbowski."

"Hello, this is Anna's friend, Michael Benson."

"Michael?"

"Yes. Anna gave me your phone number."

"Oh, yes, Michael. It's nice to hear from you."

"Would you like to meet for drinks?"

Lucy thinks for a minute. "OK. Let's meet at Café California. It has a piano bar and great food. Do you know it?"

"Yes, I do. How's eight o'clock?" says Michael.

Lucy answers, "Eight o'clock is fine. How will I know you?"

Michael says, "I'll be wearing a dark blue suit and a red striped tie."

"OK, see you at eight o'clock at Café California. Bye, Michael."

"Bye, Lucy."

# Reading Comprehension

**A**   Circle *True* or *False*.

| | | |
|---|---|---|
| 1. At first, Lucy wants to meet Michael right away. | True | False |
| 2. Michael is from Europe. | True | False |
| 3. Michael is a lawyer. | True | False |
| 4. Michael is originally from Los Angeles. | True | False |
| 5. Michael has a good job. | True | False |
| 6. Michael is quiet. | True | False |
| 7. Michael makes a small salary. | True | False |

**B**   Circle the correct answer.

1. How tall is Michael?
   a. He is short.
   b. He is medium height.
   c. He is tall.
   d. Anna didn't say.

2. Where does Michael live?
   a. in a house outside the city
   b. in an apartment in the mountains
   c. in an apartment in the city
   d. in a house downtown

3. Lucy wants to _____ Michael.
   a. meet
   b. send an e-mail to
   c. write a letter to
   d. telephone

4. How does Lucy feel about Michael? (Circle only one letter.)
   a. She's nervous and excited.
   b. She's angry.
   c. She's sad.
   d. She's hungry.

# Work with the Words

Circle the correct answer.

1. This is a **luxury** apartment building. It has _____.
   a. a bathroom in each apartment
   b. a laundry room in the basement
   c. a laundry room, a gym, a day care center, and a doorman
   d. two bedrooms, a kitchen, and a bathroom in each apartment

2. Michael is **athletic**. He likes to _____.
   a. play sports
   b. go to the movies
   c. read the newspaper and sit at home
   d. work on his computer and spend time alone

3. Her **salary** is _____.
   a. eight hours a day
   b. 40 hours a week
   c. $40,000 a year
   d. two sick days

4. In a **long-distance** relationship, two people _____.
   a. live in the same city
   b. travel together
   c. live in different cities
   d. work in different buildings

5. The opposite of **ugly** is _____.
   a. attractive
   b. not attractive
   c. talkative
   d. intelligent

6. A **gym** is a place where people can _____.
   a. read and look at magazines
   b. exercise and take exercise classes
   c. study and do homework
   d. sit and eat big dinners

7. How much does he **earn** at work?
   a. He's a computer programmer.
   b. $11.50 an hour
   c. eight hours a week
   d. many hours of overtime

**8.** My grandmother is 85 years old, but she's **in great shape**. She
_____.

   **a.** walks for an hour every day
   **b.** reads the newspaper every day
   **c.** is a wonderful cook
   **d.** loves her grandchildren

**9.** Jim is **in charge of** his department. He _____.

   **a.** is the boss       **c.** likes his job
   **b.** works there     **d.** doesn't like his job

**B**   Put the correct adjectives under each person's name. You can use some adjectives for more than one person.

| | | | |
|---|---|---|---|
| athletic | friendly | nervous | sociable |
| attractive | handsome | short | talkative |
| excited | intelligent | single | tall |

| Lucy | Anna | Michael |
|---|---|---|
| single | single | single |
| attractive | | attractive |
| | | |
| | | |
| | | |
| | | |
| | | |

Read the answers. Write the question for each answer.

How old is she?                Does she like music?
How do you know her?           Where does he live?
Where is she from?             Is she pretty?
Where does she work?

1. **Q:** *How old is she?*

   **A:** She's 25 years old.

2. **Q:** _____

   **A:** She's from Italy.

3. **Q:** _____

   **A:** He lives in the city.

4. **Q:** _____

   **A:** Yes, she does. She likes classical music.

5. **Q:** _____

   **A:** Yes, she is. She has short curly hair and blue eyes.

6. **Q:** _____

   **A:** I met her at a party.

7. **Q:** _____

   **A:** She works at a copy center.

# Lifeskill Practice

Use questions to ask about someone you don't know.
Work with a classmate. **Student A:** Cover the column on the right.
**Student B:** Cover the column on the left. **Student A:** Read the
questions on the left, and listen for the correct answer (you have it in
*italics*). **Student B:** Look at the column on the right. Listen to Student
A's question, and say the correct answer.

1. How tall is he?
   (*He's about six feet tall.*)

2. Where's he from?
   (*He's from Los Angeles.*)

3. Is he from France?
   (*Yes, he is.*)

4. How old is she?
   (*She's about 25.*)

5. How do you know him?
   (*He works in my office.*)

1. He's quiet.
   He's about six feet tall.

2. He lives in Los Angeles.
   He's from Los Angeles.

3. Yes, he is.
   He speaks English.

4. She's very nice.
   She's about 25.

5. I'm fine, thanks.
   He works in my office.

# Dialogue Practice

Practice the conversation with a classmate.

**Lucy:** Hello. Lucy Karbowski.

**Michael:** Hello, this is Anna's friend, Michael Benson.

**Lucy:** Michael?

**Michael:** Yes. Anna gave me your phone number.

**Lucy:** Oh, yes, Michael. It's nice to hear from you.

**Michael:** Would you like to meet for drinks?

**Lucy:** OK. Let's meet at Café California. It has a piano bar and great food. Do you know it?

**Michael:** Yes, I do. How's eight o'clock?

**Lucy:** Eight o'clock is fine. How will I know you?

**Michael:** I'll be wearing a dark blue suit and a red striped tie.

**Lucy:** OK, see you at eight o'clock at Café California. Bye, Michael.

**Michael:** Bye, Lucy.

# A Meeting at Café California

Episode

3

# Get Ready to Read

**A** Discuss with a partner.

1. Where is Lucy going?
2. Lucy has a date at eight o'clock. What time do you think she should arrive? Is it better to be early or late?

**B** Match the words with the definitions.

| | | | |
|---|---|---|---|
| _b_ | **1.** disappointed | **a.** | different clothes that you wear together |
| _D_ | **2.** tight | **b.** | feel sad about something that happened or didn't happen |
| _F_ | **3.** expensive | **c.** | full of people |
| _A_ | **4.** outfit | **d.** | clothes that fit close to the body; not big |
| _C_ | **5.** crowded | **e.** | not interesting |
| _G_ | **6.** late | **f.** | costs a lot of money |
| _E_ | **7.** boring | **g.** | not on time or early |

## In the last episode...

Lucy's friend, Anna, gave Lucy's phone number to a male friend. His name is Michael Benson. Anna thinks that Lucy needs to go out more. She works too hard, and she doesn't know any nice, single men. Lucy asked Anna many questions about Michael's personality, interests, height and weight, and then she agreed to go out with him. Michael called her at work, and they're going to meet at eight o'clock at Café California, a piano bar.

It's 7:30 P.M., and Lucy is getting ready to meet her blind date, Michael Benson. She's very excited, but she's very **nervous**, too. Lucy looks in the mirror to check her clothes.

**nervous**

"Am I too short? Am I wearing too much makeup? Is my dress too **tight**? Am I too young?"

The phone rings.

"Hello?" Lucy answers.

"Lucy, it's me, Anna."

"Hi, Anna. I'm getting ready. I'm glad you called. What do you want?"

"What are you going to wear?"

"I'm going to wear my black pants and my white blouse."

"What? Come on, Lucy. That **outfit** makes you look old. Wear your blue dress. It looks great on you."

"Really? Are you sure?"

"Yes, I'm sure."

"OK. Thanks for the help."

"Call me when you get home."

"I will. Bye, Anna."

"Bye, Lucy. Have a good time."

Lucy is very, very nervous. It's 7:40. She changes her clothes for the third time. Now, she's wearing a short, **simple**,* blue dress. Anna was right. The blue dress is good with her blue eyes and light brown hair. She puts on a little more makeup.

Lucy looks at her watch. It's 7:45. It's time to go. Lucy **picks up** her purse and her keys. At the door, she stops and thinks. "What am I doing? Maybe he won't be there. Maybe he's **boring**. There's a good movie on TV tonight. Maybe I will . . . But Anna knows him. He's her brother's best friend." Then she slowly opens the front door and goes to the elevator.

**pick up**

Lucy is going to meet Michael at Café California. Café California is **close**** to her building; it is only five minutes

---

*simple = not fancy
**close = not far

from her apartment, so Lucy is walking. It's a nice evening, and there are many men and women walking on the street. Lucy looks at each man. She thinks, "Is that Michael? No, he's too short. Michael's tall. Is that Michael? No, he has blond hair. Is that Michael? No, Michael has short hair. That man is very handsome, but he's **bald**."

**bald**

It's eight o'clock, and Lucy is walking into Café California. Café California is a new club in San Jose. Lucy is comfortable there because it's a friendly place. The drinks are not **expensive**, the food is good, and she likes the music very much. A band plays music on weekends, and every Monday and Wednesday a man plays the piano. It's Wednesday night.

It's 8:15, and the club is beginning to get **crowded**. Lucy orders a club soda from the bar. A very handsome man is walking towards Lucy's table, but he isn't wearing a dark blue suit. Lucy thinks, "That isn't Michael." The man passes her table and goes to a different table.

It's 8:30, and Lucy is still waiting. Michael is **late**. A tall man comes into the club. He's looking for someone. He smiles. He's smiling at Lucy! She's excited because this man is tall and handsome, but he doesn't have dark hair. He has red hair. He isn't Michael, either.

Lucy orders another club soda from the bar. She's beginning to get worried, and she's a little disappointed. Maybe Michael isn't coming. It's getting late. It's 8:45. Michael is 45 minutes late. She thinks, "He's not coming. I'm going home." She stands up and gets ready to go home.

Music begins to play. Lucy stops to listen to the piano player. It's a good song, and the singer has a nice voice. Suddenly, Lucy feels a hand on her shoulder. She turns around, and a man is looking at her. He's wearing a dark suit and a red striped tie.

"Hi! Oh, I'm so sorry I'm late. Traffic is terrible tonight. I'm very sorry."

"Michael?"

"Yes, I'm Michael. It's very nice to meet you." Lucy is very surprised. Michael isn't tall. He's short, about 5'2". His hair isn't short and wavy. It's straight, and it's very long. He doesn't look athletic. Lucy can't believe it!

"I think there's a mistake. Is your name Michael Benson?

"No, it isn't. It's Michael Cook, Susan."

Lucy says, "My name's not Susan. It's Lucy, and I'm sorry, but I'm waiting for a different person."

"I'm sorry, too, Lucy. You look nice."

Michael Cook goes to look for his date. Lucy is happy that he is not her date, but she's disappointed because Michael Benson is very late. It's nine o'clock, and she's ready to go home. Her apartment isn't far, so she's going to walk. Then a waiter walks around the bar. He's calling her name. "Phone call for Lucy Karbowski! Phone call for Lucy Karbowski!"

# Reading Comprehension

**A** Circle *True* or *False*.

1. Lucy is nervous before her date. **True** False
2. Anna likes Lucy's black pants and white blouse. True **False**
3. Café California is far from Lucy's apartment. True **False**
4. Lucy likes the café because it's expensive and has good food. True **False**
5. A band plays at the café on weekends. **True** False
6. Lucy is drinking beer. True **False**
7. Michael Cook is not very tall. True **False**
8. Lucy likes Michael Cook. True **False**

**B** Circle the correct answer.

1. How tall is Michael Benson?
   a. He is short.   **c.** He is tall.
   b. He is medium height.   d. He is very tall.

2. How tall is Michael Cook?
   **a.** He is short.   c. He is tall.
   b. He is medium height.   d. He is very tall.

3. How many drinks does Lucy order?
   a. none   **c.** two
   b. one   d. three

4. Why does Lucy think Michael Cook is her date?
   **a.** He's is wearing a dark blue suit and a red striped tie.
   b. He has long dark hair.
   c. He looks athletic.
   d. He is short, about 5 feet, 2 inches.

# Work with the Words

**A**  Match each adjective with the correct opposite.

_d_ **1.** nervous          **a.** loose; baggy

_A_ **2.** tight            **b.** far away; long distance

_i_ **3.** boring           **c.** cheap

_G_ **4.** disappointed      **d.** calm; relaxed

_H_ **5.** simple            **e.** early; on time

_F_ **6.** crowded          **f.** empty; few people

_E_ **7.** late             **g.** happy; glad

_B_ **8.** close            **h.** fancy; complicated

_C_ **9.** expensive        **i.** interesting

**B**  Complete the sentences with the correct adjectives from part A.

**1.** I didn't like the movie. It was _____.

**2.** Café California has good music, so it's very _____ on weekends.

**3.** The drinks at Café California are cheap; they're not _____.

**4.** I like my neighborhood because it is _____ to transportation.

**5.** I didn't do well on my test. I'm _____.

**6.** English is not a _____ language. The spelling is difficult.

**7.** These shoes are _____. I'm going to put on a different pair.

**8.** Don't be _____. You will do well on your test.

**9.** It's 9:15! I'm _____ for my appointment.

**C** Who says what? Write the sentences under the correct person's name.

Traffic is terrible tonight.  Call me when you get home.

That outfit makes you look old.  Oh, I'm so sorry I'm late.

Am I wearing too much makeup?  I'm sorry, but I'm waiting for a different person.

Lucy

_____

_____

Anna

_____

_____

Michael Cook

_____

_____

# Lifeskill Practice

> *Too* + adjective
>
> Lucy is very nervous about her date, so she is worried. Lucy says, "Am I too short? Am I wearing too much makeup? Is my dress too tight?"
>
> *Too* + adjective is negative.
>
> 1. This soup is *too salty*. I don't like it.
>
> 2. The classroom is *too hot*. Let's move to another room.
>
> 3. The suit is *too expensive*. I'm not going to buy it.
>
> 4. He is *too short*. He's not a professional basketball player.

Look at the pictures. Complete the sentences. Use *too* + adjective.

| cold | heavy | tall | tired |
|------|-------|------|-------|

1. Tom is _____ _____ to go to work.

2. In the winter, it is _____ _____ for the beach.

3. Jim is _____ _____ to go through the door.

4. The box is _____ _____ for the woman.

# Dialogue Practice

Practice the conversations with a classmate.

## Conversation 1

**Lucy:** Hello?

**Anna:** Lucy, it's me, Anna.

**Lucy:** Hi, Anna. I'm getting ready. I'm glad you called. What do you want?

**Anna:** What are you going to wear?

**Lucy:** I'm going to wear my black pants and my white blouse.

**Anna:** What? Come on, Lucy. That outfit makes you look old. Wear your blue dress. It looks great on you.

**Lucy:** Really? Are you sure?

**Anna:** Yes, I'm sure.

**Lucy:** OK. Thanks for the help.

**Anna:** Call me when you get home.

**Lucy:** I will. Bye, Anna.

**Anna:** Bye, Lucy. Have a good time.

## Conversation 2

**Michael:** Hi! Oh, I'm so sorry I'm late. Traffic is terrible tonight. I'm very sorry.

**Lucy:** Michael?

**Michael:** Yes, I'm Michael. It's very nice to meet you.

**Lucy:** I think there's a mistake. Is your name Michael Benson?

**Michael:** No, it isn't. It's Michael Cook, Susan.

**Lucy:** My name's not Susan. It's Lucy, and I'm sorry, but I'm waiting for a different person.

**Michael:** I'm sorry, too, Lucy. You look nice.

# Where's Michael?

# Get Ready to Read

**A** Discuss with a partner.

1. Why is Lucy at the Café California?
2. How is Lucy feeling?

**B** Match the words with the definitions.

_c_ **1.** honest

_G_ **2.** favorite

_D_ **3.** stay

_F_ **4.** blush

_A_ **5.** jealous

_B_ **6.** relax

_e_ **7.** show up

**a.** bad feeling because you want what someone else has

**b.** feel peaceful and happy

**c.** true

**d.** not leave

**e.** arrive; come

**f.** become red in the face

**g.** something that you like best

## In the last episode...

Lucy is at Café California. She arrived at eight o'clock to meet her blind date, Michael Benson. It's now nine o'clock, and the club is crowded, but Michael isn't there. Lucy is getting angry and wants to go home. She is getting her coat when a waiter begins calling her name.

**Episode 4: Where's Michael? 33**

"Phone call for Lucy Karbowski! Phone call for Lucy Karbowski!"

"I'm Lucy Karbowski."

The waiter says, "There's a phone call for you at the bar."

"Thank you."

Lucy walks to the bar. She picks up the telephone. "Hello?"

"Hello, is this Lucy Karbowski?"

"Yes, it is. Who's this?"

"Uh, Lucy . . . this . . . this is Michael Benson. I'm sorry to call you so late, but I can't come tonight."

"You can't come?"

"Yeah. I'm sorry, but uh . . . I have an important meeting."

"A meeting? Oh, is it a business meeting? It's nine o'clock."

"You're right. It is very late."

"Well . . . I'm a little disappointed. Maybe we can meet tomorrow night."

"Tomorrow night? I'm going to be busy tomorrow, too."

"Really? Well, maybe another time."

"I don't think so."

"Excuse me?" asks Lucy. She's surprised at his answer.

"Well, um . . . you see . . . Lucy, I want to be **honest** with you. I'm really sorry, but I don't have a business meeting. I'm meeting my girlfriend."

Lucy is very surprised. "What? Your girlfriend? Why did you tell my friend Anna that you were interested in meeting me?" Lucy asks.

"Because I had a fight with my girlfriend, and I wanted to make her **jealous**. But everything's OK now, and we're going to get married next summer."

"Oh, really? Well, I'm very happy for you," Lucy says, and she slams down the phone.

The **bartender** looks at Lucy. "Is anything wrong, miss?"

"No," Lucy says. "Everything's FINE! I'm leaving."

**bartender**

Lucy walks to the door to get her coat. She feels terrible and very disappointed, but she's also angry. "I can't believe I waited for one hour!" She **puts on** her coat.

Then she hears the piano playing. The music is good, and Lucy stops. She is listening to the music. The piano player is playing one of Lucy's **favorite** songs. She turns around and walks to a table near the piano. She sits down and **takes off** her coat. Lucy orders a drink from the waitress. At first, Lucy was very upset and angry, but now she's beginning to **relax**. She isn't thinking about Michael Benson. She's thinking about the music and looking at the man who is playing the piano.

"He's very good. The music is really wonderful. He's handsome, too," Lucy thinks to herself.

Lucy sits and listens to the music until eleven o'clock. It's Wednesday night, so many people are beginning to go home. She begins to talk to the piano player.

"Your music is beautiful," Lucy says.

"Thanks," he says. "I love music, and people like to listen to my music. And, of course, I love to play the piano."

"Well, you're very good."

"Thanks again. My name's Anthony, but my friends call me Tony. What's your name?"

"My name's Lucy."

"It's nice to meet you, Lucy. You look a little sad tonight. Why are you here by yourself?" Tony asks.

"Well, I . . . ," Lucy starts to say, but Tony surprises her.

"You're too beautiful to be here alone," he says. Lucy is **blushing**, and her face turns bright red. She is smiling. She looks at Tony. He's a nice-looking man. He has dark hair and dark eyes. He has a **mustache** and medium-length wavy hair. Lucy says, "Well, I came here to meet someone, but he had a problem. I heard your music and decided to listen for a few minutes. Oh, it's eleven o'clock. I have to go home." Lucy begins to get up and put on her coat.

"Wait a minute. I'm glad you **stayed**," Tony says.

puts on

takes off

mustache

"He has a beautiful smile," Lucy thinks to herself. She sits down again.

Tony continues, "The club is going to close in a few minutes. I'm really hungry. Would you like to stay and have something to eat? The food here is very good."

"I don't know . . . I have to go to work early tomorrow." Lucy thinks to herself, "What am I doing? I don't know anything about this man. He's handsome, but . . . but, he's very nice."

"Well, you have to eat, too. Come on. Take off your coat. Stay. We can talk, and I can get to know you better."

Lucy thinks about it. "Excuse me for a minute."

Lucy walks over to a window. She takes out her cell phone and calls Anna. "Hello?"

"Anna, it's me."

"Lucy? How was your date? Tell me everything."

"Michael didn't **show up**."

"He didn't show up?"

"Don't worry about it. I have a question for you. There's a very nice piano player here, and . . ."

"A piano player?"

"Yes. He's very nice, and he invited me to stay for dinner."

"Really? Is he cute?"

"Yeah, he is."

"Stay for dinner. Then call me when you get home. I want to know everything."

"OK. Talk to you later. Bye."

"Bye, bye."

Lucy returns to the table. "OK. I'll stay a little longer."

Tony smiles again. "You called a friend, didn't you?"

Lucy smiles, but she doesn't say anything.

"That's OK. I'm glad you're going to stay. I don't like to eat alone."

The bartender turns on soft music. He is putting everything away. The waiters and waitresses are cleaning the tables.

# Reading Comprehension

**(A)** Circle *True* or *False*.

1. Michael Benson is sorry.                                  **True**   False
2. Michael is married.                                        **True**   False
3. Michael is coming late.                                   True   **False**
4. After Michael calls, Lucy feels good.                     True   **False**
5. Lucy is angry at Michael Benson.                          **True**   False
6. Lucy waited for an hour.                                  **True**   False
7. Anna says Lucy should go home right away.                 True   **False**
8. Lucy's going to call Anna when she gets home.             **True**   False

**(B)** Circle the correct answer.

1. Why isn't Michael coming to the club?
   a. He doesn't like Lucy.
   b. He doesn't like Café California.
   c. He has a business meeting.
   **d.** He already has a girlfriend.

2. Why didn't Lucy leave the club?
   a. She wanted to meet a new man.
   b. Anna is coming to meet her at the club.
   **c.** She wanted to listen to the music.
   d. She wanted to have another drink.

3. Who is Tony?
   a. He's the bartender.
   b. He's a waiter.
   **c.** He's the piano player.
   d. He's the cook.

4. Right now, Lucy is going to _____.
   a. leave and meet Anna
   **b.** have something to eat with Tony
   c. make a date to go out with Tony tomorrow
   d. cook dinner for Tony

# Work with the Words

**A** Circle the correct answer.

1. Which person is **honest**?
   a. She found a ring on the street and took it to the police station.
   b. She found a ring on the street and gave it to her sister.
   c. She found a ring on the street and sold it.
   d. She found a ring on the street and took it home.

2. Tony is playing Lucy's **favorite** song.
   a. It's a new song for her, and she likes it.
   b. It's a song she knows.
   c. It's a song she knows and really likes.
   d. It's a hard song.

3. What is the opposite of "**Stay!**"?
   a. *Go away!*
   b. *Don't go.*
   c. *You're welcome.*
   d. *Thank you.*

4. Lucy **blushes** because _____.
   a. Michael didn't come
   b. Tony says she's beautiful
   c. it's cold in the restaurant
   d. she's tired

5. The husband is **jealous** because _____.
   a. his wife was talking to a handsome man
   b. his wife liked his present
   c. his wife lost her job
   d. his wife gave him a present

6. I'm **putting on** my boots because _____.
    a. it's hot
    b. it's not cold
    c. I don't like them
    d. it's raining

7. Where do you **take off** your shoes?
    a. in the classroom
    b. at airport security
    c. at restaurants
    d. in a bank

8. Where do you **relax**?
    a. at school
    b. at home on the weekends
    c. at work
    d. at the doctor's office

9. Mrs. Walker didn't **show up** for her appointment. What happened?
    a. She didn't go to her appointment.
    b. She arrived early for her appointment.
    c. She was late for her appointment.
    d. She didn't have an appointment.

**B** Complete the sentences. Use the words in the box.

| | | | |
|---|---|---|---|
| blushes | honest | puts on | stay |
| favorite | jealous | show up | take off |

1. Lucy __blushes__ because Tony says that she is beautiful.

2. At first, Michael Benson didn't tell the truth. Then he was __honest__ and told Lucy about his girlfriend.

3. Lucy __put on__ her coat because she wants to go home.

4. Michael Benson didn't __show up__ because he was with his girlfriend.

5. Michael Benson wanted to make his girlfriend __jealous__.

6. When Lucy gets ready to leave, Tony says, "__Take off__ your coat."

7. Tony plays one of Lucy's __favorite__ songs.

8. Tony wants Lucy to __stay__ and have dinner with him.

# Lifeskill Practice

*put on/take off*

Complete the sentences.

1. When it's cold, I __put on__ my sweater.
   (put on/take off)

2. When it's hot, I __take off__ my coat.
   (put on/take off)

3. I __put on__ my boots when it snows.
   (put on/take off)

4. My grandmother __put on__ her glasses to read.
   (puts on/takes off)

# Dialogue Practice

Practice the conversation with a classmate.

**Lucy:** Hello?

**Michael:** Hello, is this Lucy Karbowski?

**Lucy:** Yes, it is. Who's this?

**Michael:** Uh, Lucy . . . this . . . this is Michael Benson. I'm sorry to call you so late, but I can't come tonight.

**Lucy:** You can't come?

**Michael:** Yeah. I'm sorry, but uh . . . I have an important meeting.

**Lucy:** A meeting? Oh, is it a business meeting? It's nine o'clock.

**Michael:** You're right. It is very late.

**Lucy:** Well . . . I'm a little disappointed. Maybe we can meet tomorrow night.

**Michael:** Tomorrow night? I'm going to be busy tomorrow, too.

**Lucy:** Really? Well, maybe another time.

**Michael:** I don't think so.

**Lucy:** Excuse me?

**Michael:** Well, um . . . you see . . . Lucy, I want to be honest with you. I'm really sorry, but I don't have a business meeting. I'm meeting my girlfriend.

**Lucy:** What? Your girlfriend? Why did you tell my friend Anna that you were interested in meeting me?

**Michael:** Because I had a fight with my girlfriend and I wanted to make her jealous. But everything's OK now, and we're going to get married next summer.

**Lucy:** Oh, really? Well, I'm very happy for you!

# The Perfect Man

# Get Ready to Read

**A** Discuss with a partner.

1. Who is Lucy's perfect man?
2. Why does Lucy like Tony?

**B** Match the words with the definitions.

_f_ 1. attentive

_A_ 2. concentrate

_G_ 3. once

_D_ 4. lucky

_C_ 5. understanding

_B_ 6. anxious

_E_ 7. sleepy

a. think hard

b. excited; nervous

c. listens to other people's problems and tries to help

d. successful, maybe by accident

e. very tired; ready for bed

f. careful; thoughtful

g. one time

## In the last episode...

Lucy went to Café California for her blind date. She was nervous and excited. Anna helped Lucy choose an outfit to wear, so Lucy looked very beautiful. One problem: Lucy waited for an hour, but Michael Benson didn't show up! Then Lucy started talking to the piano player, and he invited her to have dinner with him.

It's 1:00 A.M. The telephone rings, and a **sleepy** Anna answers, "Hello?"

"Hello, Anna? Did I **wake** you **up**?"* It's Lucy.

"Lucy, what time is it? One o'clock? I **fell asleep**.** Where are you?"

"I'm at home."

"How was dinner? Tell me everything!"

"I'm tired, Anna. Let's talk tomorrow at lunchtime. I just wanted to tell you that I was home."

"OK, but tell me something. Who is he?"

"His name is Tony. He's the piano player at Café California."

"Really? I don't remember a piano player. What does he look like?"

"He has dark wavy hair and dark eyes. He has a mustache. He's really handsome."

"OK. That's good for now. Let's talk tomorrow. Good night, Lucy."

"Good night, Anna."

\*     \*     \*     \*

It's 12:30 on Monday afternoon one month later. Lucy is sitting in her office and smiling. Lucy sees Tony almost every night after work. Sometimes she meets Tony at Café California, listens to his music, and then they have dinner together. Sometimes they go out dancing. Lucy only sees Tony at night because she works during the day, but she doesn't care. Tony is wonderful, and Lucy is very happy.

*\*wake up* = stop sleeping
*\*\*fall asleep* = start sleeping

There's a **knock** on her office door.

"Come in," Lucy says.

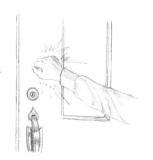

**knock**

"Hi, Lucy," Anna says. Anna knows all about Tony. Lucy is glad that she can talk to Anna about him. When Lucy first moved to San Jose, she didn't know anyone, but Anna is very talkative and very friendly, and she and Lucy quickly became friends. Anna and Lucy usually have lunch together at 12:30. "Are you ready for lunch?"

"No," Lucy says. "I didn't finish my work. I can't **concentrate**."

"Oh, really?" says Anna. "I'm not surprised. You think about Tony all day. You're thinking about him right now, aren't you?" Anna looks around the office. "Oh! Those flowers are beautiful! Are they from Tony?"

"Yes, they are."

"There were different flowers in your office last week. Does he send you flowers every day?"

"Not every day. Only **once** a week, every Monday."

"Once a week! That's expensive. I guess playing the piano is a good job."

"Well, Tony also plays in a small band, and he often plays at **weddings** on weekends. I don't know about his salary. I just know that he's wonderful, and I'm very happy."

"Well, I'm really **anxious** to meet him. When are you going to introduce me to Mr. Wonderful?" Anna asks.

"That's right. You had a cold last week, so you didn't meet Tony. **How about**[*] this Wednesday? Bring your boyfriend. We can go to Café California, and you can listen to Tony play. Then we can have a late dinner together."

"**That sounds good**.[**] Well, get back to work. I'll come back in a half hour."

---

[*]**How about** = *Let's* (We use *How about* to make a suggestion.)

[**]**That sounds good** = *OK*. (We use *That sounds good* to say *yes* to a suggestion.)

Lucy starts working. She has a picture of herself and Tony on her desk. She can't believe how happy she is. Tony is very **attentive**. He calls her every day. He sends her flowers every week. He can play piano very well, and he's also a great dancer. One night, the cook left the club early, and Tony cooked a delicious meal for Lucy. Tony is also very **understanding**. When Lucy is tired or has a problem at work, he listens to her problems. Lucy thinks that she is very **lucky**.

The phone rings. Lucy picks up the phone and answers, "Lucy Karbowski."

"Lucy! Finally! I tried to call you six times yesterday. Where were you?"

"Hello, Mom. How are you? Is everything OK?"

"Everything's fine. I left a message on your answering machine. Didn't you check it?"

"No. It was too late. I was very tired. So, **what's up?**"*

"Nothing. I just wanted to talk to you. How's work?"

"It's great."

"Do you have any new friends?"

"A few."

"Any nice men?"

"Mom!"

"Well, I'm your mother. I want to know."

When Lucy lived in Chicago with her mother, her mother always tried to introduce her to men in the neighborhood. They were doctors, lawyers, or businessman. What is her mother going to think now? "Well, I am dating a very nice man right now."

"What's his name?"

"Tony."

*__What's up?__ = *What's new?/What's happening?*

"Tony? You mean Anthony. What does he do?"

"He's a piano player. He plays at a very nice club near my apartment."

"A piano player at a club? That's not a very good job. How much does he make?"

"Mom, I don't know. I don't care about that. I make enough money!" Lucy says.

"Well, you should care, Lucy," her mother says. "I think I should meet him. I'm going to come to meet him this weekend."

"This weekend?" Lucy is speaking loudly. She's very surprised.

"Yes. I think I need to meet the piano player."

"But, Mom," Lucy says, "Don't come this weekend. I'm very busy at work right now. I have two days off next month. How about next month? We can go shopping at the new mall and spend more time together. I'm going to be very busy this weekend."

"Lucy, I'm coming this weekend. I'll call you tonight. See you soon."

# Reading Comprehension

**A** Circle *True* or *False*.

| | | |
|---|---|---|
| 1. After Lucy's dinner with Tony, she called Anna. | **True** | False |
| 2. Anna was asleep when Lucy called. | **True** | False |
| 3. Lucy is working hard today. | **True** | False |
| 4. Lucy often goes to Café California. | **True** | False |
| 5. Lucy eats lunch with Tony. | **True** | False |
| 6. Tony plays piano at weddings. | **True** | False |
| 7. Tony sends Lucy flowers every Friday. | **True** | False |
| 8. Lucy's mother thinks playing the piano is a good job. | **True** | False |

**B** Circle the correct answer.

1. This weekend, Lucy wants to _____.
   **a.** introduce Tony to Anna
   **b.** introduce Tony to her mother
   **c.** introduce Tony to her boss
   **d.** introduce Tony to all of her friends

2. Lucy and Anna usually have lunch at _____.
   **a.** 12:00          **c.** 1:00
   **b.** 12:30          **d.** 1:30

3. Yesterday, Mrs. Karbowski called Lucy _____.
   **a.** many times     **c.** twice
   **b.** once           **d.** today

4. Mrs. Karbowski is going to visit Lucy _____.
   **a.** tomorrow       **c.** this weekend
   **b.** next week      **d.** today

# Work with the Words

**A** Circle the correct answer.

1. I take my medicine **once** a day. I have to take it _____ a day.
   **a.** three times    **c.** one time
   **b.** two times      **d.** in the morning

2. My boss was very **understanding** when I arrived late. She
   _____.
   **a.** asked me if there was problem with my car
   **b.** told me to work overtime
   **c.** told me not to go out to lunch
   **d.** didn't speak to me

3. The student **fell asleep** in his class because he was _____.
   a. interested in the class
   b. very tired
   c. excited about the class
   d. worried about the test

4. You need to **concentrate** when you _____.
   a. drive
   b. eat
   c. watch TV
   d. sleep

5. Before I go to the doctor, I usually feel _____.
   a. crowded
   b. boring
   c. anxious
   d. understanding

6. Which parents are **attentive**?
   a. They don't fix good meals for their children.
   b. They help the children with their homework.
   c. They never play with their children.
   d. They don't sleep.

7. The baby is getting **sleepy**. It's time for her _____.
   a. class
   b. lunch
   c. nap
   d. bath

**B** Complete the sentences with the correct word.

| anxious | concentrate | once | understanding |
|---------|-------------|------|---------------|
| attentive | fell asleep | sleepy | wake up |

1. Tony is very _attentive_. He calls Lucy every day.

2. My friend and I go dancing every Saturday. We go dancing _once_ a week.

3. I can't _concentrate_ on my homework when the TV is on.

4. The children are very _sleepy_, so they are going to bed early tonight.

5. I always try to _wake up_ early. I like to exercise before I go to work.

6. Anna is a good friend to Lucy. When Lucy has a problem, Anna talks to her and helps her. Anna is very _understanding_

7. John worked late last night, so he _fell asleep_ in his English class.

# Lifeskill Practice

■ Everyday conversations

**A** Find the expressions in the reading. Write the page numbers.

"How about this Wednesday?" Page _____ = *Let's do it this* Wednesday.

"What's up?" Page _____ = *What's going on?*

"That sounds good." Page _____ = *That's a good idea.*

**B** Use the expressions in part A to complete the conversations.

1. **A:** I'm bored. Let's go to a movie.
   **B:** _The so_ Which movie?

2. **A:** _How_
   **B:** Nothing. What's new with you?

3. **A:** What do you want for dinner?
   **B:** _____ Chinese food?
   **A:** No. I had Chinese food last night. Let's have Italian food.
   **B:** OK. _____

4. **A:** Would you like a cup of hot chocolate?
   **B:** _____ It's cold outside.
   **A:** And _____ some cookies?
   **B:** No, thank you. I'm on a diet.

**C** Practice the conversations with a partner.

# Dialogue Practice

Practice the conversation with a classmate.

| | |
|---|---|
| **Lucy:** | Lucy Karbowski. |
| **Mrs. Karbowski:** | Lucy! Finally! I tried to call you six times yesterday. Where were you? |
| **Lucy:** | Hello, Mom. How are you? Is everything OK? |
| **Mrs. Karbowski:** | Everything's fine. I left a message on your answering machine. Didn't you check it? |
| **Lucy:** | No. It was too late. I was very tired. So, what's up? |
| **Mrs. Karbowski:** | Nothing. I just wanted to talk to you. How's work? |
| **Lucy:** | It's great. |
| **Mrs. Karbowski:** | Do you have any new friends? |
| **Lucy:** | A few. |
| **Mrs. Karbowski:** | Any nice men? |
| **Lucy:** | Mom! |
| **Mrs. Karbowski:** | Well, I'm your mother. I want to know. |
| **Lucy:** | Well, I am dating a very nice man right now. |
| **Mrs. Karbowski:** | What's his name? |

| | |
|---|---|
| **Lucy:** | Tony. |
| **Mrs. Karbowski:** | Tony? You mean Anthony. What does he do? |
| **Lucy:** | He's a piano player. He plays at a very nice club near my apartment. |
| **Mrs. Karbowski:** | A piano player at a club? That's not a very good job. How much does he make? |
| **Lucy:** | Mom, I don't know. I don't care about that. I make enough money! |
| **Mrs. Karbowski:** | Well, you should care, Lucy. I think I should meet him. I'm going to come to meet him this weekend. |
| **Lucy:** | This weekend? |

# Mother's Here!

# Get Ready to Read

**A** Discuss with a partner.

1. Why is Lucy's mother coming for a visit?
2. Is Lucy nervous about her mother's visit?

**B** Match the words or phrases with the definitions.

_d_ 1. pale

_a_ 2. chores

_g_ 3. messy

_f_ 4. full

_c_ 5. retire

_b_ 6. nosy

_e_ 7. make a good impression

a. regular household jobs

b. asks too many questions

c. stop working, usually at age 62 or older

d. has no color in the face, looks sick

e. give someone a good opinion of you

f. the feeling you have after a very large meal

g. not organized; not clean

---

☊ *In the last episode...*

Lucy thinks about Tony all the time. Anna is going to meet him this week. She's anxious to meet him because Lucy is very happy. Anna and Lucy made plans to meet at Café California, but now Lucy's mother is coming for a visit. She called Lucy and now she wants to meet Tony. Lucy is very nervous!

It's Tuesday morning, and Lucy is working from home. She has her laptop computer, and she's answering an e-mail from a coworker. Her mother is going to arrive later this afternoon, and Lucy is going to **pick** her **up**<sup>*</sup> from the airport. She's waiting for her mother to call. Early this morning Lucy cleaned her bedroom. Now she's going to **make the bed** in the guest room, **sweep** the floor, **mop** the kitchen floor, and **vacuum** the living room. Lucy's mother is arriving at about four o'clock. It's almost twelve o'clock now.

**make the bed**

Buzz. Buzz! Lucy's apartment buzzer is ringing.

"Oh, no! She's early!" Lucy says. Lucy's mother, Beata Karbowski, is always early, but today she's too early. Lucy isn't ready. There is dirty laundry on the floor in her bedroom, and the breakfast dishes are in the sink.

Buzz. Buzz! The buzzer rings again. Lucy goes to the intercom.

**sweep**

"Hello, who is it?" asks Lucy.

"It's me. Open the door! It's cold outside!"

Lucy pushes the button and opens the front door for her mother. She quickly puts the dishes in the dishwasher, and looks around the apartment. "It's not too bad," she thinks.

A few minutes later, the doorbell rings. Lucy opens the door. "Mom, it's good to see you! You're early! Why didn't you call me? I was going to pick you up at the airport."

**mop**

Mrs. Karbowski kisses and hugs Lucy. "The airport? I took the bus. Flying is too expensive."

"The bus? Mom, how long did it take?"

"Not long. Only 23 hours. I left at midnight, and I arrived at 11:15 this morning. I slept on the bus. It was very comfortable." Lucy's mother stands and looks at her daughter. "You're too thin. You look **pale**. You need to eat a good meal. Where's the kitchen?"

**vacuum**

<sup>*</sup>**pick up** someone = meet someone at the airport, train station, or after work; give someone a ride
(*pick up the phone* = answer the phone)

**Episode 6: Mother's Here! 55**

Lucy's mother always says the same thing. Lucy looks at her. "I'm fine. I'm not too thin. Why don't you relax for a few minutes? Take your coat off."

"This apartment is a mess. My home is never **messy**. Lucy, you should always keep a clean apartment. You should prepare for marriage."

"Mom, really. This is the twenty-first century! When I get married, my husband and I will both do the **chores**. And my apartment is not messy; it's clean. I was cleaning when you arrived. But you are four hours early! Come on, sit down. Relax!"

Mrs. Karbowski says, "I feel fine. I'll make you a nice lunch, and then we'll talk about your friend. What's his name? Tom?"

Lucy replies, "Tony. His name's Tony."

"OK. We'll have lunch."

Mrs. Karbowski is an excellent cook. She prepares a large lunch. They eat roast chicken, potatoes, green beans, and a salad. After lunch, Lucy is very **full**. She can't move!

**full**

"Tell me about Tony."

"Well, I met him at Café California a couple of months ago."

"At Café California? Is that a bar? You can't meet a nice man at a bar!"

"Mom, he's very nice. He's a . . ." The door buzzer rings. "Here he is now. You can meet him yourself."

A few minutes later, Tony is standing in front of Lucy's apartment door. He's a little nervous. This is the first time that Lucy is seeing him in the daytime. They always meet at night because of Lucy's job. Tony only had a few hours of sleep, so he looks a little tired. He wants to **make a good impression on** Lucy's mother, so he's wearing a new sweater, a tie, and a pair of black pants. Lucy opens the door and smiles at Tony.

"Come in, Tony. Tony, this is my mother, Beata Karbowski. Mom, this is Tony DiMarco."

Mrs. Karbowski says, "It's very nice to meet you, Timmy. Have a seat. Let's talk."

"It's Anthony, Mrs. Karbowski, but everyone calls me Tony. And it's nice to meet you, too."

Lucy and Tony sit on the sofa together. Mrs. Karbowski sits between them, and pushes Tony over a little bit. She asks him many questions. She asks him about his job, his family, his education—everything! Lucy doesn't have a chance to speak.

"Thomas," asks Mrs. Karbowski, "what are you going to do after you finish playing piano?"

"It's Tony. Well, Mrs. Karbowski," he says, "I like to play the piano. I don't have any other plans. I really like my job."

"That's very nice, Timmy," she says, "but that's not a good job for the future. How are you going to take care of a family?"

"Call me Tony, Mrs. Karbowski. When I was a child, my father played the piano, too," answers Tony. "He was a musician, and he taught my brother, sisters, and me to play instruments. He took very good care of all of us. My mother was a singer, and we were a very happy family."

"Your parents are musicians, too?"

"Well, they're going to **retire** soon, but yes, my parents are musicians. We all like music very much," answers Tony.

"How many brothers and sisters do you have?" asks Mrs. Karbowski.

"Five. I have one brother and four sisters."

"Six children? That's a large family. Lucy, I'm very tired. I think I will rest in the bedroom for a little while. It was very nice to meet you, Tommy."

"It was nice to meet you, too, Mrs. Karbowski," Tony answers.

Mrs. Karbowski goes into the other room. Lucy looks at Tony. "Tony, I'm sorry. She's only going to stay for a couple of days, and she likes to go to bed early. I'll come to see you tonight."

"OK," Tony says. "I'm going to go home and go back to bed. Your mother's very . . . interesting. Does she like me?"

"Of course she likes you," Lucy says. "She's just a little too talkative and a little **nosy**. She always asks a lot of questions. She wants to know everything."

Mrs. Karbowski calls from the bedroom. "Lucy, Lucy!"

"I'll be there in a minute, Mom. I'm saying goodbye to Tony."

"See you later, Lucy," Tony says.

Lucy kisses Tony goodbye, and he leaves. She walks into the guest bedroom. "What's wrong, Mom?"

"I want you to stop seeing that man. He's not right for you."

"What?"

# Reading Comprehension

 Circle *True* or *False*.

|  |  |  |
|---|---|---|
| 1. Lucy is working at home today. | **True** | False |
| 2. Lucy finished cleaning her apartment. | True | False |
| 3. Mrs. Karbowski is usually late. | True | False |
| 4. Lucy thinks her apartment is messy. | True | False |
| 5. Mrs. Karbowski took a bus to San Jose. | True | False |
| 6. Mrs. Karbowski thinks Lucy is too fat. | True | False |
| 7. Mrs. Karbowski brought groceries from her home. | True | False |
| 8. Mrs. Karbowski is a good cook. | True | False |

**B**  Read each question. Circle the correct answer.

1. Mrs. Karbowski is _____.
   a. talkative and nosy
   b. shy
   c. understanding
   d. messy

2. How does Tony feel today?
   a. He's tired.
   b. He's angry.
   c. He's hungry.
   d. He's tired and nervous.

3. What is Mrs. Karbowski talking about with Tony?
   a. She's asking him about his job.
   b. She's asking him about his family.
   c. She's asking him about his future plans.
   d. All of the above.

4. Tony's parents are _____.
   a. working
   b. not working anymore
   c. changing jobs
   d. opening a business

# Work with the Words

**A** Match each word or phrase with its opposite.

_e_ **1.** pale          **a.** fun activities

_d_ **2.** retire         **b.** messy

_b_ **3.** clean; in order    **c.** hungry (empty)

_c_ **4.** full           **d.** work

_a_ **5.** chores        **e.** blushing

**B** Complete the sentences with the correct words.

| | | | |
|---|---|---|---|
| chores | make a good impression | nosy | retire |
| full | messy | pale | |

1. You look _pale_. Do you have the flu?

2. My office is very _messy_. I can't find anything in it.

3. **A:** "Would you like another piece of cake?"
   **B:** "No, thank you. I'm _full_."

4. Phil is wearing a suit and tie because he wants to _make a good impression_

5. Mrs. Johnson is working now, but she's going to _retire_ next year.

6. I'd like to relax after work, but I have so many _chores_ to do at home!

7. My neighbor is very _nosy_. She always looks out the window when my doorbell rings.

**C** Read each question. Put an X under the correct name. More than one answer is possible.

| Who | Lucy | Tony | Mrs. Karbowski | Mr. and Mrs. DiMarco |
|---|---|---|---|---|
| **1.** is talkative? | | | ✓ | |
| **2.** is messy? | | | ✓ | |
| **3.** likes music? | | ✓ | | |
| **4.** is always early? | | | ✓ | |
| **5.** is attentive? | | | | ✓ |
| **6.** plays an instrument? | | ✓ | | |

# Lifeskill Practice

▨ Chores around the house

**A** Write the words next to the household chores. You can look at page 55.

_____          _____

_____          _____

**B** Make sentences about your household chores. Use the vocabulary and expressions below.

**Example:** I sweep the floor every week. I *never* vacuum.

| every day | every week | never | once a month |
|-----------|------------|-------|--------------|

# Dialogue Practice

Practice the conversation with two classmates.

| | |
|---|---|
| **Lucy:** | Come in, Tony. Tony, this is my mother, Beata Karbowski. Mom, this is Tony DiMarco. |
| **Mrs. Karbowski:** | It's very nice to meet you, Timmy. Have a seat. Let's talk. |
| **Tony:** | It's Anthony, Mrs. Karbowski, but everyone calls me Tony. And it's nice to meet you, too. |
| **Mrs. Karbowski:** | Thomas, what are you going to do after you finish playing piano? |
| **Tony:** | It's Tony. Well, Mrs. Karbowski. I like to play the piano. I don't have any other plans. I really like my job. |
| **Mrs. Karbowski:** | That's very nice, Timmy, but that's not a good job for the future. How are you going to take care of a family? |
| **Tony:** | Call me Tony, Mrs. Karbowski. When I was a child, my father played the piano, too. He was a musician, and he taught my brother, sisters, and me to play instruments. He took very good care of all of us. My mother was a singer, and we were a very happy family. |
| **Mrs. Karbowski:** | Your parents are musicians, too? |
| **Tony:** | Well, they're going to retire soon, but yes, my parents are musicians. We all like music very much. |

# Mother Goes Back Home

# Get Ready to Read

**A** Discuss with a partner.

1. Why does Mrs. Karbowski want Lucy to stop seeing Tony?
2. What do you think Lucy is going to do?

**B** Match the words with the definitions.

_b_ 1. protective

_c_ 2. professional

_f_ 3. ambitious

_e_ 4. fight

_g_ 5. break up with

_d_ 6. romantic

_a_ 7. agree

a. have the same opinion or idea

b. protect family, friends, or other people from bad situations

c. have a job that needs special training: doctor, teacher, lawyer

d. do special things for spouse, girlfriend or boyfriend

e. argument; angry discussion

f. want to do better in a job or other situation

g. end a relationship

## In the last episode...

Mrs. Karbowski traveled 763 miles from Portland, Oregon, to San Jose because she wanted to meet Lucy's boyfriend, Tony. Mrs. Karbowski asked Tony many questions. Lucy was nervous about her mother's visit. Tony was nervous, too, but he talked about his job and his family. His parents are musicians, too. Mrs. Karbowski was not happy. She told Lucy to stop seeing Tony.

Lucy is very upset. She can't believe her mother. Lucy thinks Tony is a wonderful person. He's very nice to other people. He's very understanding, and he's **romantic**. He sends her flowers every week! Mrs. Karbowski thinks that Tony is a nice person, but Tony is not the right man for Lucy. Mrs. Karbowski doesn't like musicians because she thinks they don't make good salaries. She wants Lucy to meet a **professional** man: a doctor, a lawyer, or an engineer. Lucy and her mother are having a big **fight** about Tony. Now, Lucy is crying. She wants her mother to like Tony, but Mrs. Karbowski wants Lucy to stop seeing him. She wants Lucy to **break up with** him!

"I know that you like Tony," Mrs. Karbowski says, "but what about the future? Is he going to marry you? Are you going to take care of the family? You have an excellent job. Do you want to take care of him?"

"Mom, that's not important!" Lucy says. "Dad didn't have an office job, but he took very good care of us."

"Don't talk about your father," Mrs. Karbowski says. "That was different. Your father didn't have a good education or a good job, but he was very hardworking. He never took a vacation. He only worked and worked. Then he had a **heart attack**[*] when he was only 40 years old and left me alone with two children. I want something better for you, Lucy."

"I know, Mom," says Lucy, "but I want to marry someone I love."

"You can love a professional man with a college education and a good office job," said Mrs. Karbowski. "Stop seeing Tony before it's too late."

"What do you mean?"

"I mean stop seeing him before you fall in love with him," Mrs. Karbowski says.

"It's too late," Lucy says quietly.

"You're in love with him?"

"Yes, I am."

"Well, you have to **break up with** him. Don't see him anymore," Mrs. Karbowski says.

"But Mom, Tony is a wonderful person."

"Lucy. I'm not going to say this again. Stop seeing him." Mrs. Karbowski starts putting on her coat.

[*]**heart attack** = a serious medical emergency when a person's heart stops

"Where are you going?" asks Lucy.

Mrs. Karbowski is picking up her suitcase. "I think I'll go home now."

"But it's 23 hours on the bus! Please stay!"

Mrs. Karbowski thinks for a moment. "OK, Lucy. I'll leave tomorrow. We can talk about this tonight."

A few minutes later, the telephone rings. It's Tony.

"Lucy? Where are you?"

Lucy is **whispering**,* "Oh, Tony. I'm so upset. My mother doesn't want me to see you anymore."

"Why not?"

"I'll tell you tomorrow. My mother's going to leave tomorrow. I'll come to see you after work."

"Are you going to break up with me?" Tony asks.

"Of course not. Just wait. My mother will change her mind."

"I hope so."

"I'm sure she will. I'll see you tomorrow." Lucy hangs up the phone.

\*     \*     \*     \*

When Mrs. Karbowski gets back to Portland the next day, she telephones her son, Paul, who also lives in Portland. Paul and Lucy are very close, and they try to see each other every few months. Paul is Lucy's older brother, and he's very

---

*whisper = speak in a very soft voice

**protective** of his baby sister. He helped her buy a car. He also helped her choose a college. Lucy always calls Paul when she has a problem.

Paul looks like Lucy, and he's tall and hardworking like his father, but he's different, too. He's very **ambitious**. He is an investment banker and works at a large international bank. He works long hours, often works weekends, and earns a very good salary.

Mrs. Karbowski tells Paul about Lucy and Tony. Paul **agrees** with his mother. He thinks Lucy should meet a professional man.

"Mom, why don't I fly down to San Jose and visit with Lucy? I can introduce her to my friend Max. You remember him, don't you? He was my college roommate, and he lives in San Jose, too. He's an engineer."

"When can you introduce them?"

"I'll call Max today and invite him to dinner. I'll bring Lucy with me."

"Perfect. Call me when you get back."

"OK. Bye, Mom."

"Bye, sweetheart."

\*   \*   \*   \*

It's 7:00 P.M. the next day, and Lucy is excited. Paul is coming for a visit this weekend. She can't wait to see him. (Paul didn't tell her about Max.) They're very close, and they're best friends. She wants Paul to meet Tony. She knows that Tony and Paul will be good friends.

# Reading Comprehension

**A**  Circle *True* or *False*.

1. Mrs. Karbowski likes Tony very much.                True    **False**
2. Paul gets a good salary.                            **True**    False
3. Mrs. Karbowski is understanding.                    True    **False**
4. Mr. Karbowski was a lawyer.                          True    **False**
5. Mr. Karbowski took good care of his family.         **True**    False
6. Mr. Karbowski worked very hard.                      **True**    False
7. Mr. and Mrs. Karbowski had three children.          True    **False**
8. Lucy's brother wants to meet Tony.                   True    **False**

**B**  Circle the correct answer.

1. Mr. Karbowski died _____.
   a. in a car accident            c. in an accident at work
   **b.** of a heart attack        d. at an old age

2. Mrs. Karbowski doesn't like Tony because _____.
   a. he is too old                c. he is not a nice person
   b. he is too rich               **d.** he is not a professional man

3. Paul is _____.
   a. a college professor          c. a car salesman
   **b.** an investment banker     d. an airplane pilot

4. Paul is coming to San Jose _____.
   a. on a business trip
   b. because Lucy invited him
   **c.** because he wants to talk to Lucy
   d. to meet Tony

# Work with the Words

**A** Circle the correct answer.

1. The two children were crying because they both wanted the same toy, and they had a _____ about it.
   a. conversation
   b. heart attack
   c. talk
   d. fight

2. Sam is not **ambitious**. He doesn't _____.
   a. want to go home early
   b. want a promotion
   c. want to have days off
   d. want to take breaks

3. Sometimes teenagers and their parents don't _____ about clothes.
   a. break up
   b. agree
   c. whisper
   d. fall in love

4. Ronald is very **romantic**. On his wife's birthday, he _____.
   a. worked late at the office
   b. gave her flowers and took her to a special restaurant
   c. took her to a fast food restaurant
   d. gave her a toaster

5. Rosa is **protective** of her children. They never _____.
   a. do homework
   b. go to the park alone
   c. eat good food
   d. wear coats in the cold weather

6. Lucy's mother wants her to marry a _____ man with a good salary.
   a. professional
   b. romantic
   c. nosy
   d. sleepy

**B** Complete the sentences with the correct word.

| agree | break up with | professional | romantic |
|-------|---------------|--------------|----------|
| ambitious | fight | protective | whisper |

1. Paul Karbowski is a very successful banker. He's a
   _professional_.

2. I am very _ambitious_. I work more than forty hours a week
   plus overtime every weekend.

3. Lucy and her mother had a ___fight___ about Tony.

4. Susan's boyfriend is very _romantic_. He cooked a special
   dinner for her on her birthday. He put candles on the table and
   decorated the room.

5. My brother and his wife are very different, but they
   ___agree___ about important things. They have the same
   ideas about their children.

6. My sister wants to _break up with_ her boyfriend. He works all
   the time, so he doesn't have time for her. Also, he forgot her
   birthday.

7. Shh! You should _whisper_. The baby is sleeping in the next
   room.

8. Leo is very _protective_ of his children. He doesn't let them
   walk to school alone, and he always makes them call him before
   they are ready to come home from school.

# Lifeskill Practice

**Family discussions**

Many parents and children, especially teenagers, have different opinions about many things. "I agree" means that you have the same opinion; "I disagree" means that you have a different opinion.

**Example: Father:** Your boyfriend is not good for you.
  **Daughter:** I disagree.
  (a.) He is very attentive.
  **b.** He never listens to me.
  **c.** He doesn't help me with my homework.

**A** Complete the following conversations. Circle the correct responses. Then practice the conversations with a partner.

1. **Mother:** You stay out too late.
   **Daughter:** I disagree.
   **a.** I am always home before 2:00 A.M.
   **b.** I am never home for dinner.
   **c.** I always call you and tell you where I am.

2. **Son:** I need a part-time job.
   **Mother:** I agree.
   **a.** You can work 40 hours a week.
   **b.** You don't need to work.
   **c.** You can work a couple of hours after school.

3. **Daughter:** I need a new car. All my friends have new cars.
   **Father:** I disagree.
   **a.** A used car will be fine.
   **b.** A new car is cheap.
   **c.** I will buy you a new car tomorrow.

**B** PAIRS. Write a new conversation with a partner. Use *agree* or *disagree*.

# Dialogue Practice

Practice the conversations with a partner.

### Conversation 1

**Tony:** Lucy? Where are you?

**Lucy:** Oh, Tony. I'm so upset. My mother doesn't want me to see you anymore.

**Tony:** Why not?

**Lucy:** I'll tell you tomorrow. My mother's going to leave tomorrow. I'll come to see you after work.

**Tony:** Are you going to break up with me?

**Lucy:** Of course not. Just wait. My mother will change her mind.

**Tony:** I hope so.

**Lucy:** I'm sure she will. I'll see you tomorrow.

### Conversation 2

**Paul:** Mom, why don't I fly down to San Jose and visit with Lucy? I can introduce her to my friend Max. You remember him, don't you? He was my college roommate, and he lives in San Jose, too. He's an engineer.

**Mrs. Karbowski:** When can you introduce them?

**Paul:** I'll call Max today and invite him to dinner. I'll bring Lucy with me.

**Mrs. Karbowski:** Perfect. Call me when you get back.

**Paul:** OK. Bye, Mom.

**Mrs. Karbowski:** Bye, sweetheart.

# Paul's Plan

# Get Ready to Read

**A** Discuss with a partner.

1. Why is Paul coming to San Jose?
2. What does Lucy want to tell her brother?

**B** Match the words with the definitions.

_b_ 1. ethnic food    **a.** not busy

_f_ 2. pick up    **b.** food from different countries

_a_ 3. free    **c.** make a good impression on someone

_g_ 4. have a seat    **d.** person, not family, who lives in the same apartment or house

_c_ 5. impress

_d_ 6. roommate    **e.** not interested

_e_ 7. bored    **f.** give someone a ride

   **g.** sit down

## In the last episode...

Two nights ago, Lucy and her mother had a big fight about Lucy's boyfriend, Tony. Mrs. Karbowski doesn't think that Tony is the right man for her daughter. She wants her daughter to marry a more professional man, not a piano player or a musician. When Mrs. Karbowski got home, she called her son, Paul. He also lives in Portland. She told him about Lucy's boyfriend. Paul agrees with his mother, so he's going to San Jose to visit Lucy. He has a plan. He's going to introduce Lucy to one of his friends, but Lucy doesn't know anything about it!

Paul? Max. I'm in town to see my sister. Are you free for dinner tonight?

Paul Karbowski is on an airplane in the first class section. He's flying from Portland, Oregon, to San Jose, California, to visit his sister, Lucy. Two nights ago, Lucy and her mother had a big fight about Lucy's boyfriend, Tony. Mrs. Karbowski called Paul and asked him to talk to Lucy. Paul thinks that his mother is right, and now he's on his way to see Lucy. He has a plan.

Paul is going to take his little sister, Lucy, out to dinner tonight. Lucy doesn't know that Paul invited his college roommate, Max, to come to dinner, too. Lucy thinks that Paul is coming for a business meeting. She and her brother are very close, so she can't wait to see him. She wants to tell him about Tony. Paul has another idea. Paul invited Max because he thinks that Max is the right man for Lucy. Max is an engineer, and he lives near Lucy in San Jose.

A few hours later, Paul calls Lucy from his hotel room. "Hi, Lulu! I'm here in San Jose. What time do you want to have dinner?"

"Paul, I'm glad you're here. I have a lot to tell you. I'll come to your hotel in an hour," says Lucy. She is excited to see her brother.

"No, Lulu," Paul says, "I'll come to your apartment and **pick** you **up**. I have a rental car. I'll see you in an hour."

"Great," says Lucy. "See you in an hour."

An hour later, Lucy and Paul are in a restaurant downtown. They're waiting in line. They're laughing and having a good time. The restaurant is crowded and noisy, but Lucy and Paul don't have to wait because Paul made a reservation.

The hostess asks, "Name, please?"

"Karbowski," Paul answers.

"This way, please."

When Lucy sees that they have a table for four, she says, "Paul, we don't need a big table. We can wait for a smaller one."

"This is fine," Paul says to the hostess.

"Your waiter will be here in a minute," says the hostess.

Lucy and Paul sit down. "Why do we need a big table, Paul? There are only two of us."

Paul looks to the door, stands up, and says, "Max! Over here!"

A nice-looking man, medium height with blond hair, comes over to their table. "Hi, Paul! It's good to see you again," he says.

Lucy is surprised. She's **wondering**,* "Who is this?"

"Lucy, this is Max Cooper. Max, do you remember my sister, Lucy? Lucy, this is Max, my **roommate** from college. **Have a seat**, Max.

"Uh, it's nice to see you again, Max."

"It's nice to see you too, Lucy. The last time I saw you was a long time ago. You were in high school. You look very different now." Max sits next to Lucy. "Your brother always talks about you, Lucy."

"Oh, really? What does he say?" asks Lucy.

"Oh, he says that you are beautiful and very intelligent."

Lucy blushes bright red. "Really?"

"Would you like something to drink?" asks Paul. Paul calls the waiter over to the table.

"Hello, my name is Robert. I'll be your waiter tonight. May I get you something to drink?" the waiter asks.

*__wonder__ = ask yourself, think

Paul looks at his sister. "What would you like, Lucy?"

"I'll have a club soda with lime, please," Lucy tells the waiter.

"I'll have the same," Paul answers. "How about you, Max?"

"Make that three club sodas," Max tells the waiter.

The waiter writes the order, and says, "I'll be right back with your drinks."

Paul and Max begin talking. Lucy is quiet. She is thinking to herself. "Hmm. This is strange. Paul knows that I want to talk to him about Tony. Why is Max here? Paul didn't tell me he invited Max to dinner. What's going on? Did he talk to Mother?"

"You know, Lucy," says Paul, "You and Max are both in San Jose. Did you know that?"

"No, I didn't know that, Paul."

"You're both single, and you are both professionals. Maybe you and Max can be friends. You know, Lucy, you don't know many people here."

"Yes, Lucy," says Max. "I hear that you're new in this area. This is my hometown. I can show you all the fun places to go. Do you enjoy dancing? I know all of the best clubs in San Jose. Do you like **ethnic food**? I know all of the best Mexican restaurants in San Jose and a great Vietnamese place. Do you like soccer? My company has season tickets."

Max and Paul are talking and talking and talking. Max is good-looking, but Lucy is not interested in him. She's **bored**. She isn't enjoying herself. She wants to go to Café California and meet Tony, but she doesn't have her car because Paul picked her up. Suddenly, a cell phone rings.

"Excuse me," Paul says, "I have to call my office."

A few minutes later, Paul returns. "Lulu, I'm so sorry. I have to go back to my hotel and make an important business call. There's an emergency at my office."

"I'll go with you," Lucy quickly stands up to leave.

"No, no," Paul says. "You don't have to go. Enjoy yourself. I'll pay for dinner. Max, could you take my sister home?"

"Sure, no problem," Max says. "Call me tomorrow, Paul. Let's have lunch before you go back."

"Good idea. Lulu, I'll call you later." Paul kisses his sister on the cheek and leaves.

Max continues to talk about himself and his job. He makes a lot of money, and he is trying to **impress** Lucy, but Lucy is not impressed. She doesn't want to stay with Max. She wants to go home right away. "Max, can you take me home? I don't feel well."

"Sure, Lucy," Max says. "Let's go."

A few minutes later, Lucy and Max are in front of her apartment building. He gets out of the car to open her door, but Lucy is already out of the car.

"Thank you, Max," Lucy says. "It was nice to see you again."

"Nice to see you, too," Max says. "You really are a beautiful and intelligent woman. I would like to go out with you again. Are you **free** tomorrow?"

Lucy puts out her hand to shake Max's hand. "Sorry. I'm busy. Good night. I have to go."

Suddenly, Max grabs Lucy's hand and pulls her close to him. He kisses her. Lucy is trying to push him away when she sees a man standing across the street.

"Tony!" Lucy says. She pushes Max away.

It's Tony. He looks very angry and gets into his car. "Wait! Tony, wait!" Lucy shouts and runs down the street, but Tony is driving too fast. Lucy stands on the sidewalk and watches his car turn the corner.

# Reading Comprehension

**A** Circle *True* or *False*.

| | | |
|---|---|---|
| 1. Paul is driving to San Jose. | True | **False** |
| 2. Paul is Lucy's older brother. | **True** | False |
| 3. Paul and Lucy have a good relationship. | **True** | False |
| 4. Lucy knows that Max is coming to dinner. | True | **False** |
| 5. Max and Lucy were in high school together. | True | **False** |
| 6. Max knows San Jose very well. | **True** | False |
| 7. Lucy thinks Max is interesting. | True | **False** |
| 8. Lucy wants to stay at the restaurant. | True | **False** |

**B** Circle the correct answer.

1. The restaurant is _____ .
   a. crowded
   b. quiet
   c. noisy
   **d. both a and c**

2. Lucy is _____ to meet Max.
   a. happy
   b. angry
   **c. surprised**
   d. very happy

3. Lucy thinks that Paul talked to _____ .
   a. Tony
   **b. their mother**
   c. their father
   d. Anna

4. When Tony saw Lucy and Max together, he _____ .
   a. introduced himself to Max
   **b. became angry and drove away**
   c. thought that Max was her brother
   d. waited for Max to leave

**Episode 8: Paul's Plan  79**

**C** Put the events in order from 1 to 9.

___2___ Mrs. Karbowski called Paul.

___4___ Paul and Lucy went to a restaurant.

___7___ Max took Lucy home.

___3___ Paul decided to introduce Lucy to his friend Max.

___6___ Paul got a phone call and left the restaurant.

___1___ Mrs. Karbowski didn't like Tony.

___5___ Max came to the restaurant and Paul introduced him to Lucy.

___9___ Tony saw Lucy and Max together. He drove away.

___8___ Max kissed Lucy.

# Work with the Words

**A** Circle the correct answer.

1. Max and Paul were **roommates** in college. They _____.
   a. lived in the same room
   b. lived next door to one another
   c. attended the same university
   d. studied in the same class

2. Lucy is **bored** because _____.
   a. Max is very interesting and fun
   b. Max is not interesting to her
   c. Max doesn't like her
   d. she has a cold

3. New York is full of many restaurants that serve **ethnic food**. Visitors can eat _____.
   a. only American food
   b. only hot dogs and hamburgers
   c. Chinese and Mexican food
   d. Chinese, Thai, Italian, and other kinds of food

4. Mr. Robinson wanted to **impress** the manager at his job interview. He wore _____.

   a. sneakers and jeans

   b. dirty jeans and a T-shirt

   c. jeans, a tie, and old shoes

   d. a suit, a tie, and new shoes

5. *I'm free for breakfast Thursday at 8:30* means: _____

   a. I can eat breakfast with you.

   b. I can't eat breakfast with you.

   c. I don't have to pay for breakfast.

   d. You have to pay for breakfast.

6. Bus passenger 1: "Is anyone sitting here?"
   Bus passenger 2: "No, _____."

   a. you can't sit here

   b. have a seat

   c. you can sit over there

   d. the bus is full

7. The students are getting ready to take a test. One very serious student is **wondering** _____

   a. "What's for dinner?"

   b. "What time is the break?"

   c. "Is it going to rain today?"

   d. "Is the test going to be difficult?"

8. Carlos **picked up** Joe because _____.

   a. Joe's car was not working well

   b. Joe's car was in good condition

   c. Carlos didn't know how to drive

   d. Joe wanted to ride his bicycle

# Lifeskill Practice

■ Ordering in a restaurant.

**(A)** Read and practice the conversation with three classmates.

| | |
|---|---|
| **Waiter:** | May I get you something to drink? |
| **Customer 1:** | I'll have a cup of coffee with milk. |
| **Customer 2:** | I'll have an iced tea. |
| **Customer 3:** | Make that two iced teas. |
| **Waiter:** | Thank you. I'll be right back with your drinks. |

**(B)** Write and practice a new conversation.

# Dialogue Practice

Practice the conversation with your classmates.

| | |
|---|---|
| **Hostess:** | Name, please. |
| **Paul:** | Karbowski. |
| **Hostess:** | This way, please. |
| **Lucy:** | Paul, we don't need a big table. We can wait for a smaller one. |
| **Paul:** | (*to the hostess*) This is fine. |
| **Hostess:** | Your waiter will be here in a minute. |
| **Lucy:** | Why do we need a big table, Paul? There are only two of us. |
| **Paul:** | Max! Over here! |
| **Max:** | Hi, Paul! It's good to see you again. |
| **Paul:** | Lucy, this is Max Cooper. Max, do you remember my sister, Lucy? Lucy, this is Max, my roommate from college. Have a seat, Max. |
| **Lucy:** | Uh, it's nice to see you again, Max. |
| **Max:** | It's nice to see you, too, Lucy. The last time I saw you was a long time ago. You were in high school. You look very different now. Your brother always talks about you, Lucy. |
| **Lucy:** | Oh, really? What does he say? |
| **Max:** | Oh, he says that you are beautiful and very intelligent. |
| **Lucy:** | Really? |
| **Paul:** | Would you like something to drink? |

# The Breakup

# Get Ready to Read

**A** Discuss with a partner.

1. What happened to Lucy? Why is she upset?
2. Why didn't Tony stay and talk to Lucy?

**B** Match the words with the definitions.

| | | | |
|---|---|---|---|
| _d_ | **1.** confused | **a.** | alone and not happy about it |
| _f_ | **2.** take someone out | **b.** | use up; not have any more |
| _g_ | **3.** furious | **c.** | sad; no energy |
| _b_ | **4.** run out of | **d.** | doesn't understand |
| _a_ | **5.** lonely | **e.** | become thinner |
| _c_ | **6.** depressed | **f.** | pay for someone's meal |
| _e_ | **7.** lose weight | **g.** | very angry |

## In the last episode...

Lucy went to dinner with her brother, Paul. She didn't know that Paul also invited his college roommate, Max. Paul wanted Lucy and Max to meet. He agrees with their mother; he thinks Lucy and Tony should break up. Lucy didn't know about Paul's plan. Max was handsome, but Lucy was not interested in Max; she thought he was boring. Paul left dinner early to make an important business call. Lucy wanted to leave and meet Tony, so she said she didn't feel well. She didn't have her car, so Max took her home. In front of her apartment building, Max told Lucy that he wanted to see her again, and he kissed her. Tony saw them!

"Tony!" Lucy shouts. "Tony! Come back!"

Max is **confused**. "Who was that?" he asks.

"That was my boyfriend," Lucy says. She's very upset.

"Boyfriend? I didn't know that you had a boyfriend. Your brother didn't say anything about a boyfriend," Max says. "I'm leaving. This situation is too **complicated**\* for me."

Max gets into his car and drives away. Lucy goes upstairs to her apartment. She sits down on the sofa and calls Tony's cell phone. The phone rings, but the voicemail picks up, "Hi, this is (408) 555-2880. Please leave a message at the beep."

Lucy hangs up. She tries a few more times, but Tony doesn't answer.

An hour later, the phone rings. "Tony?" Lucy says quickly. "No, this is Paul, Lulu," he says. "So, how was your date with Max? He's a great guy, isn't he? He's perfect for you."

"No, he isn't, Paul. And we didn't have a date. You left me alone with him at the restaurant. You know that I'm interested in another man. I wanted to talk to you about Tony and introduce you. Did you talk to Mom?"

"Well, . . . yes, I did. I think she's right. You need a professional man—not a piano player," he says.

"You don't know what I need, Paul. I'm **furious** with you! Tony came to see me tonight, and he saw Max try to kiss me!"

"Good," says Paul. "Maybe now you'll find a better man. Max is perfect for you."

"Perfect for me? Are you **nuts**?\*\* Max talked about himself all through dinner. He is in love with himself," Lucy says and she hangs up the telephone. Then she tries to call Tony again, but his answering machine picks up. Lucy decides to leave a message: "Tony, this is Lucy. Please talk to me. I know you're at home. The man that you saw me with was a friend of my brother's. I'm not

\*****complicated** = not simple, difficult, not easy to understand

\*\***nuts** = crazy

interested in him. He kissed me. I didn't kiss him. I love you, Tony. Please . . ." BEEP! The answering machine **runs out of** time.

*　*　*　*

Two weeks later, Lucy is at her office. She isn't happy. It's lunchtime, but she isn't hungry. She's not eating, and she's **losing weight**. She is very **lonely** because she **misses**[*] Tony. She tried to talk to Tony at Café California, but Tony didn't want to talk to her. When he saw Lucy, he walked away. She telephones Tony two or three times a day, but he doesn't answer her calls. Lucy is **depressed**.

Lucy's office phone rings. "Hello, Lucy Karbowski."

"Lulu? It's me, Paul."

"Paul, I'm busy. I can't talk to you now," Lucy starts to hang up the phone.

"Wait, Lucy. Don't hang up. Talk to me. I'm sorry."

"What?"

"I'm sorry, Lucy. You're right. I invited Max to dinner. I talked to Mom, and she told me everything."

"That's right. You were wrong, Paul. You didn't meet Tony. He's a wonderful guy."

"OK. I'll give him a chance. I'll come to visit this weekend, and I'll **take** both of **you out** to dinner."

"Too late, Paul. Tony's not talking to me. He's mad at me."

"Why?"

"Because your friend Max tried to kiss me in front of my building. Tony saw me with Max."

"Oh, don't worry about that. He'll forget about it. Call me when things are good again, OK?"

[*]**miss** = feel sad because someone or something is not there

"OK. Bye, Paul."

"Bye, Lulu."

Lucy hangs up the phone and tries to do some work. She calls Tony again, but there's no answer. She checks her cell phone for messages, but there's only one message—from her mother. Lucy does not want to talk to her mother. Then, someone knocks on her office door.

It's Anna. "Lucy? Are you in there? Let's go to lunch. It's 12:30."

"I'm not hungry," says Lucy, but she opens the door.

"Lucy, you look terrible. You have to eat something." Anna tries to make Lucy feel better. "I know a new Japanese restaurant in the neighborhood. Come on. It's a beautiful day."

"No. I don't want to. Maybe Tony will call," Lucy says. She looks at her telephone.

"Lucy, you tried to talk to him for two weeks. You're a wonderful person, and you didn't do anything wrong. Forget about Tony," Anna tells her friend.

"I don't want to forget about him. He was wonderful. He was understanding. He was perfect for me," Lucy starts to cry.

"Fine. Stay by the phone. Hey! I have an idea. Why don't you go to his apartment and wait for him? He has to go home sometime. Maybe if he sees you again, he might listen to you."

"That's a great idea! I'll go to his apartment tonight. He usually gets home after midnight. I'll take a taxi and wait until he comes home," Lucy says. She is beginning to smile. "I know he'll talk to me."

Lucy tries to work, but she can't concentrate. All she can think about is Tony. Maybe he will listen to her.

\*   \*   \*   \*

It's **midnight**, and Lucy is getting out of a taxi in front of Tony's apartment. "Thank you," Lucy says to the taxi driver. "My boyfriend will be home in a few minutes. I'll be fine."

The taxi driver is a little worried because it's late, it's dark, and the street is empty. "Are you sure, miss?" he asks.

**midnight**

"I'm sure," Lucy says. The taxi driver stays in his cab for a few minutes. Lucy sits on the steps to Tony's building and waits.

A few minutes later, she sees someone coming down the street. When the taxi driver sees the man, he drives away. Lucy stands up. "Tony?" she says.

It's a man, but it isn't Tony. This man has long dirty hair, and he looks messy. Lucy is a little nervous. She starts looking in her purse. She's pretending to look for a key.

"Good evening, can I help you?" he says.

"No, thank you," Lucy says nervously. "I'm waiting for someone. He's going to be here soon."

"Why don't you wait with me?" the man asks. "I live around the corner." The man is making Lucy more nervous.

"No, thank you," Lucy says nervously, and she walks to the steps and sits down again. Suddenly, the man grabs her **purse**.

"Hey!" Lucy shouts. "Leave me alone! Help!"

The man tries to take Lucy's purse, but Lucy pulls away. She starts screaming, "Help! Somebody help! Leave me alone!" She pulls away and hits the man with her purse.

"Ow!" the man yells. He pushes her, and Lucy falls down on the sidewalk and hits her head on the steps.

The man takes Lucy's purse, opens it, takes her wallet and starts to look for jewelry. Lucy is lying on the ground.

"Hey! What are you doing?" someone shouts. A man comes running. It's Tony!

# Reading Comprehension

**A** Circle *True* or *False*.

1. Before the dinner, Max knew that Lucy had a boyfriend.      True    **False**

2. After dinner, Max wanted to see Lucy again.      True    **False**

3. Paul talked about Tony with his mother.      **True**    False

4. Lucy is angry at Paul.      **True**    False

5. Tony wants to talk to Lucy.      True    **False**

6. Lucy is looking for a new boyfriend.      True    **False**

7. Lucy is losing weight because she is sick.      True    **False**

8. At first, Anna thinks that Lucy should forget about Tony.      **True**    False

**B** Circle the correct answer.

1. Lucy feels _____.
   a. sad
   b. lonely
   c. excited
   **d. a and b**

2. Lucy looks _____.
   a. hungry
   b. beautiful
   **c. terrible**
   d. nervous

3. When Paul called Lucy the second time, he _____.
   a. wanted her to see Max again
   **b. was sorry**
   c. didn't want to meet Tony
   d. wanted her to move to Portland

**Episode 9: The Breakup 89**

**4.** The taxi driver doesn't want to leave Lucy at Tony's building because _____.

    **a.** it's too early

    **b.** it's raining

    **c.** he is a friend of Lucy's

    **d.** it's very late and it's dark

**C** What happens to Lucy in front of Tony's apartment building? Complete the paragraphs with the words in the box. You don't need every word.

| | | | | |
|---|---|---|---|---|
| are | dark | drives away | messy | purse |
| arrives | dirty | early | midnight | Tony |
| ambitious | driver | is | Paul | worried |

**1.** Lucy _____is_____ waiting for _____Tony_____ to come home. The taxi _____driver_____ is waiting, too. He is _____worried_____ because it is _____dark_____, and the street is empty. A strange man _____ambitious_____. He is _____dirty_____ and _____messy_____. Lucy's taxi _____drives away_____

| | | | | |
|---|---|---|---|---|
| arrives | hits | leaves | purse | taxi |
| down | is | lying | pushes | Tony |
| driver | jewelry | nervous | talks | wallet |
| help | late | Paul | | |

**2.** At first, the man is friendly, and he _____talks_____ to Lucy. Then he tries to take Lucy's _____purse_____. Lucy yells for _____help_____, and _____hits_____ the man with her purse. The man _____pushes_____ Lucy, and she falls _____down_____. She is on the sidewalk. The man opens Lucy's purse and takes her _____wallet_____. He also looks for _____jewelry_____. Then another man _____arrives_____. It's _____Tony_____!

# Work with the Words

1. I am **confused** when _____.
   a. I know all the answers on a test
   **b.** I don't understand the homework
   c. I understand everything
   d. a test is easy

2. Mr. Banks was **furious** because _____.
   a. his employees did good work
   b. his employees were on time for work
   c. his employees were late again
   d. his employees worked very hard

3. Susan was **depressed** when _____.
   a. she found $20 in her pocket
   b. she received an A on her test
   c. she received a new car
   d. she didn't get the job that she wanted

4. I'm trying to **lose weight**, so I am _____.
   a. eating more sweets
   b. not eating vegetables
   c. eating less and exercising more
   d. watching more TV and eating potato chips

5. English spelling is **complicated** because _____.
   a. it's easy to spell
   b. the sounds and spelling are the same
   c. it is the same as my native language
   d. the sounds and spelling are different

6. Maria was **lonely** because _____.

    **a.** her friends came to visit

    **b.** she had many friends

    **c.** her best friend moved away

    **d.** her boyfriend moved to her state

7. Our teacher had to go to his office because he **ran out of** _____.

    **a.** paper

    **b.** candy

    **c.** money

    **d.** water

8. I want to visit my family in my country because _____.

    **a.** I miss them

    **b.** I'm furious

    **c.** I want to take them out

    **d.** I'm confused

## Lifeskill Practice

*run out of*

Lucy can't leave a message because Tony's answering machine runs out of time. We use *run out of* for many things.

Complete the sentences with the words in the box. You don't need every word.

| energy | gas | milk | money | paper |
|---|---|---|---|---|

1. I need to go to the grocery store. We ran out of ____milk____.

2. The printer doesn't work. It ran out of ___paper___.

3. We have to stop at the next service station. We're going to run out of ___gas___.

4. I stopped going to that fancy new gym because I ran out of ___money___.

# Dialogue Practice

Practice the conversation with a classmate.

**Lucy:** Hello, Lucy Karbowski.

**Paul:** Lulu? It's me, Paul.

**Lucy:** Paul, I'm busy. I can't talk to you now.

**Paul:** Wait, Lucy. Don't hang up. Talk to me. I'm sorry.

**Lucy:** What?

**Paul:** I'm sorry, Lucy. You're right. I invited Max to dinner. I talked to Mom, and she told me everything.

**Lucy:** That's right. You were wrong, Paul. You didn't meet Tony. He's a wonderful guy.

**Paul:** OK. I'll give him a chance. I'll come to visit this weekend, and I'll take both of you out to dinner.

**Lucy:** Too late, Paul. Tony's not talking to me. He's mad at me.

**Paul:** Why?

**Lucy:** Because your friend Max tried to kiss me in front of my building. Tony saw me with Max.

**Paul:** Oh, don't worry about that. He'll forget about it. Call me when things are good again, OK?

**Lucy:** OK. Bye, Paul.

**Paul:** Bye, Lulu.

# Back Together

# Get Ready to Read

**(A)** Discuss with a partner.

1. Why did Lucy go to Tony's apartment?
2. What happened to Lucy?

**(B)** Match the words with the definitions.

_d_ 1. weak

_g_ 2. concussion

_a_ 3. concerned

_f_ 4. headache

_e_ 5. hurt

_c_ 6. fill out

_b_ 7. rob

a. worried

b. steal from someone

c. write information, usually on forms or applications

d. not strong

e. injured

f. pain in the head, usually not serious

g. a serious injury to the head

## In the last episode...

Lucy was upset because Tony did not answer her phone calls. Anna told her to go to Tony's apartment and wait for him after work. Lucy took a taxi to Tony's apartment. It was very late, and the street was dark. A strange man came and tried to take her purse. The man was trying to take Lucy's wallet and jewelry. He pushed Lucy, and she fell down and hit her head. Then Tony arrived!

🎧 "Call 911! Help! Someone's **hurt**! Call 911!" Tony is shouting in the street. It's after midnight. Suddenly, lights begin coming on in the building. Residents are looking out their windows. Lucy is lying on the ground in front of the building. Her eyes are closed. Tony is talking to Lucy. "Lucy, Lucy! Open your eyes! Please wake up. Look at me, Lucy."

Lucy begins to open her eyes, "Umm. Uh . . . what happened? Where am I?"

"Lucy!" Tony cries. "You're **awake**.* Thank goodness! I was so worried. How do you feel?"

"Tony?"

"Yes, Lucy. I'm here. What are you doing here? It's after midnight."

Lucy says, "Tony, I'm OK." She tries to stand up, but she falls down again. Tony catches her.

"Lucy, stay where you are. You need help."

Lucy is speaking very quietly. "You didn't answer my phone calls. You didn't talk to me. I wanted to see you. I wanted to explain . . ."

"Don't talk, Lucy," Tony says. "You're hurt. Lucy, the police are coming. Here's the ambulance. They're going to take you to the hospital."

Lucy begins to sit up. "I don't need to go to the hospital."

"Be quiet. You're going to the hospital. You have a cut on your head. You're bleeding!"

Thirty minutes later, Tony and Lucy are sitting in the emergency room of the hospital. They're waiting to see a doctor. The desk clerk gives Lucy some papers. "Could you please **fill out** this form?"

Lucy sits down and begins to fill out her medical history. She is feeling better, but Tony looks a little worried.

"I think I should call your mother," Tony says.

"No. Don't call her. She'll worry. I'll call her when I get home. I'm feeling much better," Lucy says.

"Are you sure? You look pale." Tony looks upset and very **concerned**. worried

"Tony, relax. I have a **headache**, but I feel OK. Really. I'm fine." Lucy tries to make Tony feel better, "Tony, I want to talk about Max."

"Don't talk. You need to rest."

A clerk calls Lucy's name, "Lucy Karbowski!"

*awake = not sleeping

**96** *Lucy and the Piano Player*

Tony helps Lucy walk to the counter. Lucy is **weak**, so she is walking very slowly. "I'm Lucy Karbowski."

"The doctor is ready for you. Please follow me." Tony walks with Lucy to the door to the examining room, but the clerk stops him.

"Sir, are you family?" asks the clerk.

"No, I'm not. I'm her boyfriend," says Tony.

"I'm sorry, sir. You'll have to wait here. I'll help her," says the clerk. The clerk takes Lucy into the examining room. Tony sits down and waits. He's too nervous to sit, so he stands up and begins to **pace**\* around the room.

Lucy is sitting on a table in the examining room. A doctor comes in.

The doctor looks at a chart, "Miss . . ."

"Karbowski," Lucy says to the doctor.

"Miss Karbowski. I'm Dr. Patel. So, what happened to you?"

"Well, I was waiting for my boyfriend, and a man tried to **rob** me. He pushed me down, and I think I hit my head on the sidewalk. There's a cut on my head, back here." Lucy is pointing to the back of her head.

"How do you feel?" the doctor asks. She's looking at the cut on the back of Lucy's head.

"I had a bad headache, but I feel better now."

"I'm going to bandage that cut and examine you. You might have a **concussion**, but I think we can send you home tonight. You're very lucky."

"Yes, I am," says Lucy. She's thinking about Tony.

About an hour later, the desk clerk tells a very nervous Tony that he can go into the examining room. "Your friend is waiting for you," says the clerk.

\***pace** = walk back and forth, usually when you are nervous

Tony goes into the examining room and sees Lucy. A nurse is helping Lucy stand up. She has a bandage around her head, but she smiles at him. "How is she?" Tony asks the nurse.

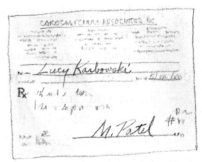

prescription

"She'll be fine. Dr. Patel gave her a **prescription** and bandaged the cut on her head. She needs rest," says the nurse.

"I'll take her home right now."

"Sir, someone needs to stay with her tonight. She can't stay alone. She has a small concussion," the nurse says. "Are you family?"

"Not exactly. I'm her boyfriend. I'll make sure that she's OK," Tony says.

Lucy is smiling at Tony.

"Lucy, you look much better. How are you feeling?" Tony asks.

"Tony, stop worrying. I'm fine. Dr. Patel was very nice. She said that I can go home now. I want to tell you about Max and my brother."

"Not now, Lucy. You need to rest."

"No, Tony. Now. Listen. Max is my brother's friend. They were roommates in college. Paul and I went to dinner together, and he wanted me to meet Max. I didn't know anything about it. Max met us at the restaurant. He gave me a ride home. He wanted to go out with me again, but I didn't want to go out with him. I didn't . . . He kissed me! I didn't kiss him. I pushed him away!"

"Lucy. Relax, honey. I understand. I was upset, but I'm OK now. I was jealous, but I know that you aren't interested in that guy. Please calm down. You're getting upset."

"I don't need a doctor, Tony. You're the only medicine I need." Lucy and Tony hug.

When Lucy and Tony leave the examining room, two police officers are waiting outside. One police officer says, "Miss Karbowski, we need to ask you some questions."

# Reading Comprehension

**A** Circle *True* or *False.*

|   |   | | |
|---|---|---|---|
| 1. | Tony calls 911. | True | False |
| 2. | The neighbors wake up. | True | False |
| 3. | Tony is angry at Lucy now. | True | False |
| 4. | Lucy can talk. | True | False |
| 5. | Lucy goes to the police station. | True | False |
| 6. | Lucy needs medical treatment. | True | False |
| 7. | Lucy has to stay in the hospital overnight. | True | False |
| 8. | Lucy calls her mother right away. | True | False |

**B** Circle the correct answer.

1. Who is waiting to talk to Lucy when she leaves the examining room?
   **a.** a doctor          **c.** the police
   **b.** her mother        **d.** a nurse

2. After Dr. Patel sees Lucy, Lucy _____.
   **a.** feels much better    **c.** is very nervous
   **b.** is very sick         **d.** begins to cry

3. In the waiting room, Tony is _____.
   **a.** relaxed              **c.** sure that Lucy is going to be OK
   **b.** nervous and worried  **d.** angry and upset about Max

4. Lucy wants to talk to Tony about _____.
   **a.** her future with him  **c.** her brother, Paul
   **b.** her family           **d.** her brother, Paul, and his friend Max

**C** Put the events in order from 1 to 8.

_2_ Tony stops the robbery.

_4_ The ambulance arrives.

_7_ Tony talks to the nurse.

_1_ Someone tries to rob Lucy.

_5_ Lucy goes to the hospital.

_3_ The man runs away.

_8_ Lucy tells Tony about Max.

_6_ Lucy sees a doctor.

# Work with the Words

**A** Circle the correct answer.

1. It's 2:00 in the morning and Richard is **awake**. He can't _____.
   a. do his homework
   **b.** sleep
   c. eat
   d. drink

2. Jessica is **concerned** about her grades because _____.
   a. she is doing very well on her tests
   b. she is getting high grades
   c. she doesn't have time to study
   d. the tests are easy

3. Mr. Jackson begins to **pace** in the waiting room because _____.
   a. he is hungry
   b. he is relaxed
   c. he is happy
   d. he is nervous

4. When I have a **headache**, I _____.
   a. go to the hospital
   b. go to the beach
   c. take aspirin
   d. eat a hamburger

5. I got a _____ because someone tried to **rob** me.
   a. new television
   b. new lock
   c. lot of money
   d. new doorbell

6. The opposite of **weak** is _____.
   a. tired
   b. interesting
   c. delicious
   d. strong

7. When I went to the personnel office, I **filled out** _____.
   a. a letter
   b. an application
   c. my car
   d. my name

**B** Complete the sentences with the correct word.

| awake | concussion | hurt | rob |
| concerned | headache | prescription | weak |

1. **Mother:** Johnny, why are you still __awake__? It's late, and you have school in the morning!
   **Johnny:** Sorry, Mom. I'm going to bed right now.

2. **Officer:** What happened?
   **Man:** Someone tried to __rob__ me. I think he took my wallet.
   **Officer:** Can you describe the person?

3. **Mrs. Lopez:** What's the matter? You're so pale, and you look terrible.
   **Mr. Lopez:** I have a bad __headache__. I'm going to go to bed early.

4. **Doctor:** Please take this __prescription__ to your pharmacy. Take the medicine twice a day.
   **Patient:** Thank you, Dr. Green.

5. **Mr. Kelly:** Dr. Green, does my son have a __concussion__? He hit his head on the car window.
   **Dr. Green:** Let me check.
   **Mr. Kelly:** Thank you.

6. **Dr. Green:** How about you, Mr. Kelly? Were you __hurt__ in the accident?
   **Mr. Kelly:** No, I wasn't, Dr. Green. I was wearing my seat belt.

7. **Teacher:** Mrs. Lopez. Would you like to see your daughter's tests?
   **Mrs. Lopez:** Yes, please. I'm very __concerned__ about her schoolwork.
   **Teacher:** Don't worry. She's doing fine.

8. **Mrs. Smith:** Are you OK? You look pale.
   **Mr. Smith:** I feel a little __weak__. I think I'm getting the flu.
   **Mrs. Smith:** Go to bed early.

# Lifeskill Practice

■ Medical vocabulary

Complete the sentences with the correct word.

> concussion    headache    hurt    nurse    prescription

1. Mr. Collins worked on his computer all day. Now he has a _concussion_.
2. The _nurse_ took my temperature and blood pressure.
3. I am lucky. I wasn't _hurt_ in the car accident.
4. Lucy fell down and hit her head. She has a small _headache_.
5. You can fill a _prescription_ at the drugstore.

# Dialogue Practice

Practice the conversation with your classmates.

## Conversation 1

**Clerk:**  Lucy Karbowski!

**Lucy:**  I'm Lucy Karbowski.

**Clerk:**  The doctor is ready for you. Please follow me. Sir, are you family?

**Tony:**  No, I'm not. I'm her boyfriend.

**Clerk:**  I'm sorry, sir. You'll have to wait here. I'll help her.

## Conversation 2

**Tony:**  How is she?

**Nurse:**  She'll be fine. Dr. Patel gave her a prescription and bandaged the cut on her head. She needs rest.

**Tony:**  I'll take her home right now.

**Nurse:**  Sir, someone needs to stay with her tonight. She can't stay alone. She has a small concussion. Are you family?

**Tony:**  Not exactly. I'm her boyfriend. I'll make sure that she's OK. Lucy, you look much better. How are you feeling?

**Lucy:**  Tony, stop worrying. I'm fine. Dr. Patel was very nice. She said that I can go home now. I want to tell you about Max and my brother.

**Tony:**  Not now, Lucy. You need to rest.

# A Surprise

# Get Ready to Read

 **A** Discuss with a partner.

1. Why are Lucy and Tony at the hospital?
2. What questions are the police officers going to ask Lucy and Tony?

**B** Match the words with the definitions.

_e_ 1. interrupt
_d_ 2. flight
_a_ 3. embarrassed
_f_ 4. take care of
_g_ 5. unfortunately
_c_ 6. arrest
_b_ 7. hobby

a. nervous, uncomfortable, ashamed, especially in front of other people

b. something that people do regularly for fun: a sport, read books, work in the garden, etc.

c. police take a person away because they think the person did something illegal

d. airplane trip

e. stop someone else's conversation by speaking

f. be responsible for someone, especially a sick person, older person, or child

g. a pity; too bad

---

## In the last episode...

Lucy was lucky. Tony arrived, and the strange man ran away. He took Lucy's wallet, but he didn't have time to take her jewelry. Lucy fell and hit her head, but she only had a headache and small concussion. The ambulance took her to the hospital. At the hospital, a doctor examined her, gave her a prescription, and told her to go home. Tony was very worried. Now he is taking Lucy to her apartment. They are ready to leave the hospital, but two police officers are waiting for them.

At the emergency room, Lucy and Tony stop to answer questions from two police officers, Officer Martinez and Officer Chang. "We'd like to ask you some questions, Miss Karbowski. Could you have a seat over here, please?"

Officer Chang points to two chairs in the waiting area. It's about 2:30 in the morning, and the emergency room is quiet.

Officer Martinez begins, "Tell me, Miss Karbowski, what time did you arrive at the address on First Street?"

Lucy answers, "It was about midnight."

Officer Martinez asks, "Why were you out so late?"

Lucy is quiet. Then she says, "I was waiting for my boyfriend. I wanted to talk to him."

Officer Chang asks, "Why didn't you call him on the phone?"

Tony **interrupts**, "Is that important, Officer?" He looks a little **embarrassed**.

Officer Martinez looks at Tony and says, "Yes, it is, sir. Please don't interrupt."

Tony looks at Lucy and says, "Sorry."

Officer Martinez says, "So, Miss Karbowski, tell me what happened."

Lucy tells the officers her story again. Officer Chang takes notes. Finally, Officer Martinez says, "We have some good news for you. We found your wallet, and we **arrested** the **mugger**,* and he's in jail now. His name is Rick Remo. He is usually in that neighborhood, and we believe that he robbed another woman last week. He was only a few blocks away. He was looking through your wallet."

"That's great," says Lucy, "I was worried about my identification. When can I get my wallet?"

Officer Chang answers, "**Unfortunately**, we have to keep your wallet as **evidence**,** but we will give you your driver's license and credit cards."

---

*mugger = criminal who attacks and robs people in the street
**evidence = object or information that can be used legally (in court) to prove something

**lineup**

**identify**

"Thank you, Officer. That's great news," says Tony.

"You're welcome, sir," says Officer Martinez.

"Can we go now?" asks Tony. "My girlfriend has a small concussion and a terrible headache. She needs rest."

"Yes, you can go, but we will need you to come down to the police station later this morning to **identify** the mugger in a **lineup**.

"Oh? Can he come with me?" Lucy points to Tony.

"Yes, miss. You can bring your friend with you. You can go home now. Thank you."

"Good night, Officer," says Lucy. Lucy and Tony leave.

It's five o'clock in the morning when Lucy and Tony finally arrive at Lucy's apartment. Lucy unlocks her door and turns on the light. Anna is sleeping in a living room chair. She wakes up right away.

"Lucy, are you OK?" Anna hugs Lucy a little too tightly. Anna is upset.

"Ouch! That's too tight. What are you doing here?"

"Tony called me. He had your cell phone. Hi, Tony. It's nice to meet you."

Tony shakes Anna's hand. "It's nice to finally meet you, too, Anna. Lucy needs to take her medicine and get some rest."

"Of course. Sit down, Lucy. I'll get you a glass of water."

Tony and Anna are trying to make Lucy comfortable. They both look a little concerned.

"Relax, you guys. I'm fine," Lucy says. "I just need to sleep."

"Of course," says Tony, "I'm going to go home now. I'll call you in the later."

"Don't leave, Tony. I'll feel better with both of you here."

"OK. We'll stay in the living room," says Anna. Anna takes Lucy back to the bedroom. When Anna comes back, she says to Tony, "Now, Tony. Tell me everything."

Later that morning, at about nine o'clock, Anna, Tony, and Lucy are in the kitchen having tea. Everyone is very tired because no one slept well. The doorbell rings. Anna says, "I'll get it." She goes to the door and pushes the intercom. "Who is it?" She listens and says, "It's your mother and brother, Lucy." Anna buzzes them in.

"What are they doing here?" asks Lucy. "I'm too tired for another fight."

Tony says, "They're here? Good. I called them, Lucy."

When Anna opens the door, Mrs. Karbowski runs to her daughter. "Lucy! Thank goodness you're all right."

"I'm fine, Mom. Tony is taking care of me. What are you doing here?" Lucy isn't happy to see her family. Paul looks surprised. "Tony called Mom, and she called me. We went to the airport and took the first **flight** here. We arrived thirty minutes ago." Paul looks at Tony and shakes his hand, "Thank you for calling us."

"Paul, this is Tony, my boyfriend. You didn't give me an opportunity to introduce you. You talked to Mom and decided that Tony was not good for me."

Paul asks. "Mom, do you know who this is?"

"Yes, he's a piano player at a bar," she says. Mrs. Karbowski is feeling more relaxed now.

Lucy is tired, but she's angry, too. "Mom, Tony is my boyfriend, and this is my home. Be nice to him. You, too, Paul."

Anna is watching everything. She asks, "Mrs. K. would you like some tea? How about you, Paul?"

Paul shakes his head. He's **staring**[*] at Tony.

[*]**stare** = look at something or someone very carefully for a long time

"That would be nice, Anna. I'm sorry, Lucy," says Mrs. Karbowski. "I'm worried about you."

"Don't worry about me. My friends are **taking** good **care of** me."

"Are you sure?" asks her mother. "He's . . . "

Paul interrupts. "Mom, do you know who this is? This is Anthony DiMarco!"

"I know, Paul. He's dating your sister."

"But you don't understand, Mom. I read an article in a business magazine about Tony's family. I saw Tony's picture in the magazine! His family's company **makes** pianos. They make pianos for famous musicians, orchestras, and concert halls!"

Lucy looks confused. "Is that true, Tony?"

Tony looks embarrassed and answers, "Yes, it is, Lucy."

"But why didn't you tell me?"

"Well, Lucy, I wanted to make sure that you loved me for myself—not for my money. Playing the piano is just a **hobby** for me. I play the piano for fun because I love to do it. In the daytime, I work for my family's company. That's why I never meet you in the daytime. I often fly to other cities for meetings. Now I know that you love me, not my family's money. Lucy, I wanted to . . . "

Mrs. Karbowski interrupts. "Lucy, I made a mistake. I think a piano player will make the perfect son-in-law." Mrs. Karbowski is smiling.

"Future wife? Son-in-law? Tony, what are you saying?" Lucy asks.

Tony pulls a ring out of his pocket. "Lucy, when I saw you with Max, I had this ring in my pocket. That's why I was so upset. I know that we only met a few months ago, but I hope that you will say 'Yes.'"

Lucy puts her arms around Tony. "Yes! Yes! Yes!"

Anna is smiling. "Well, this is Mr. Wonderful."

Mrs. Karbowski says, "I'll make breakfast. All of you look too thin."

# Reading Comprehension

**A** Circle *True* or *False*.

1. Lucy answers the police officer's questions.     True    **False**
2. The mugger is in jail.     **True**    False
3. The police are giving Lucy back her wallet.     True    **False**
4. Lucy has to go to the police station later.     **True**    False
5. Anna is very worried about Lucy.     **True**    False
6. Paul takes Lucy home.     True    **False**
7. Anna called Lucy's mother and brother.     True    **False**
8. Lucy wants to see her mother and brother.     True    **False**

**B** Circle the correct answer.

1. How do Lucy, Anna, and Tony feel in the morning?
   - **a.** embarassed
   - **b.** disappointed
   - **c.** upset
   - **d.** tired

2. When Lucy's family arrives, Lucy _____.
   - **a.** is happy to see them
   - **b.** is too tired for a fight
   - **c.** makes tea for them
   - **d.** goes back to bed

3. Paul knows Tony's face because _____.
   - **a.** he saw Tony's picture in a magazine
   - **b.** they work together
   - **c.** they met at Café California
   - **d.** Lucy introduced them at the restaurant

4. Mrs. Karbowski likes Tony now because _____.
   - **a.** Tony has a large family
   - **b.** Tony can play the piano
   - **c.** Tony's family has a large business
   - **d.** he is Lucy's boyfriend

**C**  Who said it? Write the name of the character.

| Anna | Mrs. Karbowski | Paul |
|------|----------------|------|
| Lucy | Officer Martinez | Tony |

1. It's nice to finally meet you.           _____

2. Thank you for calling us.                 _____

3. Tell me everything.                        _____

4. Why were you out so late?                 _____

5. I was worried about my identification.    _____

6. He's a piano player at a bar.             _____

7. We'd like to ask you some questions.      _____

8. I'll feel better with both of you here.   _____

**D**  REVIEW: Write answers to the questions.

1. What does Lucy do?

   _____

   _____

   _____

   _____

   _____

2. What does Tony's family do?

   _____

   _____

   _____

   _____

   _____

**3.** Why didn't Mrs. Karbowski like Tony in the beginning?

_____

_____

_____

_____

**4.** What happened to Lucy in front of Tony's building?

_____

_____

_____

_____

**5.** What did Dr. Patel do at the hospital?

_____

_____

_____

_____

# Work with the Words

**A** Circle the correct answer.

1. The teenager was **embarrassed** because _____.
   a. he received a good grade on his test
   b. his parents gave him a new cell phone
   c. he received the lowest grade in his class
   d. he got a promotion at his job

2. Lucy is going to the police station to **identify** _____.
   **a.** a police officer     **c.** a mugger
   **b.** her car            **d.** Tony

3. A _____ takes care of patients.
   **a.** nurse        **c.** police officer
   **b.** teacher      **d.** banker

4. We want to get married outside. **Unfortunately,** _____.
   **a.** it's not going to be cold
   **b.** it's going to rain
   **c.** it's going to be a beautiful day
   **d.** it's going to be sunny and warm

5. At first I didn't know the man, but I remembered his name after I _____ him for a long time.
   **a.** embarassed     **c.** stared at
   **b.** arrested        **d.** took care of

6. I have a **hobby**. I like to _____.
   **a.** travel and take photos
   **b.** work overtime
   **c.** sleep eight hours a day
   **d.** eat breakfast

7. _____ **arrested** the mugger.
   **a.** A neighbor      **c.** Tony
   **b.** Mrs. Karbowski   **d.** The police officers

**B**   Complete the sentences with the correct word. You do not need all the words.

| | | | |
|---|---|---|---|
| Anna | doesn't want to | medicine | the police officers |
| arrested | evidence | Mrs. Karbowski | sleeping |
| arrives | flight | mugger | tight |
| cell phone | happy | nervous | tired |

1. Lucy and Tony are at the hospital. Lucy _doesn't want to_ call her family right away, but Tony uses Lucy's _cell phone_ and calls everyone from the waiting room of the hospital. Before they leave the hospital, _the police officers_ ask Lucy some questions. The officers tell Lucy that they _arrested_ the _mugger_ near Tony's apartment building.

2. Anna is _sleeping_ in a chair when Lucy and Tony get back to her apartment. Anna is very _nervous_ and hugs Lucy. Then she gets Lucy a glass of water. Lucy takes her _medicines_ and goes to bed. Then Tony tells _Anna_ everything. The next morning, everyone is very _tired_. Lucy's family _arrives_ early because they took the first _flight_ to San Jose.

**C** WORD SEARCH PUZZLE: Read the definitions and circle the words.

1. very angry
2. talks a lot
3. not interested
4. make money
5. _____ time; not busy
6. Tony is a piano _____.
7. the opposite of *neat* or *clean*

8. A woman carries her things in this.
9. Lucy lives in _____ Jose.
10. Lucy works at a _____.
11. not understanding
12. Lucy's best friend
13. He's mad at Lucy.
14. the opposite of *late*

```
S S E E M O E E M A U
C P U R S E N E E N N
L L R B U O S E S N R
E A N N A U O S A A R
D Y E Y O N N Y Y L L
U E V I T A K L A T K
V R R U L S F R E E T
N U N O Y S N A U A F
F Y O A B N R E C A A
D E S U F N O C P R O
U L N R U F U T F B E
```

# Lifeskill Practice

■ Crime vocabulary

Write the words next to the pictures.

arrest     evidence     identify     lineup     mugger

_____

_____

_____

_____

# Dialogue Practice

Practice the conversation with your classmates.

## Conversation 1

**Officer Martinez:** Tell me, Miss Karbowski, what time did you arrive at the address on First Street?

**Lucy:** It was about midnight.

**Officer Martinez:** Why were you out so late?

**Lucy:** I was waiting for my boyfriend. I wanted to talk to him.

**Officer Chang:** Why didn't you call him on the phone?

**Tony:** Is that important, Officer?

**Officer Martinez:** Yes, it is, sir. Please don't interrupt.

**Tony:** Sorry.

**Officer Martinez:** So, Miss Karbowski, tell me what happened.

## Conversation 2

**Officer Martinez:** We have some good news for you. We found your wallet, and we arrested the mugger, and he's in jail now. His name is Rick Remo. He is usually in that neighborhood, and we believe that he robbed another woman last week. He was only a few blocks away. He was looking through your wallet.

**Lucy:** That's great. I was worried about my identification. When can I get my wallet?

**Officer Chang:** Unfortunately, we have to keep your wallet as evidence, but we will give you your driver's license and credit cards.

**Tony:** Thank you, Officer. That's great news.

**Officer Martinez:** You're welcome, sir.

```
S S E E M O E E M A U
C P U R S E N E E N N
L L R B U O S E S N R
E A N N A U O S A A R
D Y E Y O N N Y Y L L
U E V I T A K L A T K
V R R U L S F R E E T
N U N O Y S N A U A F
F Y O A B N R E C A A
D E S U F N O C P R O
U L N R U F U T F B E
```